8 5 4

PUBLIC
POLICY

The Conservation Foundation is a nonprofit research and communications organization dedicated to encouraging human conduct to sustain and enrich life on earth. Since its founding in 1948, it has attempted to provide intellectual leadership in the cause of wise management of the earth's resources.

PUBLIC POLICY
for
CHEMICALS

National and International Issues

Sam Gusman, Konrad von Moltke,
Frances Irwin, and Cynthia Whitehead

The Conservation Foundation

Contents

Chapter IV—Notification Requirements   57

Chapter V—Risk Assessment and Control   79

Foreword

Across the world, tens of thousands of chemicals are being manufactured and marketed; yet only a small fraction of these have been tested for their long-term effects on the environment and human health. This situation has sometimes aroused the public's fear—fear that, given the known hazards from a few chemicals, we may be more seriously at risk than we know from many chemical substances in commerce. We are already aware of the effects caused by chlorofluorocarbons, asbestos, benzene, and PCBs and contemplate an ever-larger list of commercial chemicals with severe health effects.

Has technology unleashed powerful, long-term processes that will seriously injure human health or degrade the habitability of the planet? There is no realistic way to allay our fears, which may or may not prove to be well founded, short of evaluating commercial chemicals to determine whether they are, in fact, hazardous or not. Once suitable tests are performed, assessments of risk can be made, and decisions taken on measures to control those risks judged to be unreasonable.

As is the case for many environmental issues, the time has come to move toward intensive study of the scientific, technical, and political issues raised by the proliferation of commercial chemicals. The products of science and technology have created opportunities for great good. We should not abandon our efforts to improve the quality of life and to use technology in a manner that respects and cooperates with the enduring processes of nature. These efforts require that we recognize the likelihood that some chemicals will cause injury if their potential for harm is either not known or not respected. It is this awareness that has led nations to examine increasingly the adverse effects of chemicals—and the appropriate control of such effects.

These issues must be addressed in each nation by publicly accountable decision makers—though there is also general agreement that manufacturers of potentially hazardous products have direct responsibility to develop information to assess risks of injury, and are liable for injuries caused by their products. The fine balancing of public control and private initiative in developing and commercializing chemical products is dealt with in the Toxic Substances Control Act in the United States, as well as in the Directive 79/831/EEC of the European Community, and in national laws of several European nations and Japan. We can confidently expect that many other nations will enact legislation dealing with these matters and that there will be serious and active efforts to implement these laws during the years ahead.

Environmental distribution of chemicals does not respect national boundaries. And virtually every kind of product traded internationally contains chemicals or products derived from their use. No nation is immune from the consequences of its trading partners' decisions. Together with the authors, we believe that an awareness of these international factors will help develop more effective national policies, as countries throughout the world decide how they will deal with the important issues of notification, testing, and control as a vital step toward dealing with the hazards of chemicals.

—William K. Reilly, President   —Edgar Faure, Chairman of the Board
   The Conservation Foundation   Institute for
                                          European Environmental Policy

Preface

The control of risks to human health and the environment due to commercial chemicals is increasingly the subject of national law and regulation. Some of those who develop policies are keenly aware of the international ramifications of their actions. Yet we think that the circle of people who understand the international context of such matters is still quite small, and that it needs to grow rapidly because of the speed with which important issues are being decided. The purpose of this book is to assist interested members of the public, businessmen, government officials, and legislators in understanding national and international aspects of chemical control issues.

We view this book as a primer on notification, testing, and control of chemicals. It is an overview rather than a detailed treatise. Our approach is to present the subject in a manner emphasizing the interrelationships among major topics, so that the reader can see choices for action within a broad framework. In this sense, we hope to contribute to discussion of the issues and, more importantly, to informed decision making.

We have emphasized developments in the United States and in the Member States of the European Community, where events are moving at a rapid pace and, we believe, are forming a major point of reference for future legislation and regulation, worldwide, in this field. For this reason, and also because time and resources required that we limit our scope, we have only dealt lightly with the situation in other chemical-producing countries, such as Japan, except as related to the important discussions under way in the Organisation for Economic Cooperation and Development (OECD). Also, we have not dealt with the special problems of nations that do not produce chemicals or are just beginning to do so; these deserve separate attention and serious examination, yet depend significantly on the kinds of issues discussed here.

This book is a cooperative effort of The Conservation Foundation of Washington, D.C., and the Institute for European Environmental Policy of

Bonn. As the joint effort of American and European institutions, the primer incorporates issues and points of view considered important on each side of the Atlantic.

Between 1969 and 1979, Canada, Denmark, France, Japan, Norway, Sweden, Switzerland, the United Kingdom, and the United States enacted laws to control toxic substances. In September 1979, the European Community adopted a Directive concerning procedures to be followed before marketing new chemical substances. This Directive will have to be transformed into national law by September 1981 in the Member States of the Community.

Even if laws in different countries share a common purpose—protection of public health and the environment—dissimilar national approaches toward testing and notification of new chemicals, risk assessment and control, and treatment of confidential business information may create nontariff barriers to trade in chemicals and products derived from chemicals. Because of trade and the distribution of chemicals in our environment, decisions by any nation on assessing and controlling risk may affect other countries and, in some cases, the international community as a whole. Many individuals who have been closely involved in the initial drafting and implementation of chemical control policies are just now beginning to perceive some of these possibilities.

As national controls take shape in the 1980s, knowledge of the consequences of national differences of approach will help assure that those differences, if any, that ultimately prevail are chosen by nations on the basis of mutual understanding of each other's positions and of the international implications of national choices.

It would seem pointless for different nations inadvertently to take divergent paths toward toxic substances control if a common path would facilitate their mutual efforts toward public health, environmental protection, and economic well-being. Thus, we have emphasized opportunities for harmonization of national approaches. Yet decisions to control toxic substances are made in administrative, political, and cultural contexts that may differ enormously from one country to the next. What will work in one context may appear nearly impossible in another. We have given special attention to these differences.

In developing the issues for presentation, we drew heavily on expert advice in two principal ways. First, experts from the United States and Europe were asked to prepare papers on five key issues in toxic substances control: notification, testing, risk assessment and control, international trade, and information transfer. Second, papers by these contributing authors were used as background for discussions by an Advisory Committee whose members were chosen on the basis of their breadth of experience and involvement in these matters. The Advisory Committee brought together knowledgeable people from legislative and executive branches of national governments, the European Community, the Organisation for Economic Cooperation and Development, the chemical industry, and public interest groups. Members of the committee served only as individuals expressing their personal views, not the official views of any organization or government. The Advisory Committee met at the Chateau de Maffliers in Montsoult, France, at the end of November 1979; we have drawn heavily on the discussions at that meeting.

We are deeply indebted to all of the contributing authors and members of the Advisory Committee for giving so freely of their time and knowledge. Their thoughts and language are woven into the text of this manuscript. While the opinions and policy options presented here reflect the views expressed in the background papers and during the course of Advisory Committee discussions, no attempt was made to achieve consensus. Rather, the contents of this book express the best current judgments of the four authors, recognizing that many of the issues are in flux.

We are particularly grateful to the various organizations that have contributed in different ways to the funding of this project. Support came in part from The George Gund Foundation. The European Cooperation Fund in Brussels supported the meeting of the Advisory Committee in November 1979. The German Federal Ministry of the Interior also provided financing for the project, as well as for the translation into German of the manuscript. The National Audubon Society provided a portion of the funds for printing the English edition. Partial funds have also been contributed by The Conservation Foundation and the Institute for European Environmental Policy. In addition, in the fall of 1980 the Environmental Protection Agency sponsored a U.S. meeting to discuss implementation of TSCA as it is influenced by international events in toxic substances control. The primer formed part of the materials for that meeting. To this end, EPA has provided partial support for the development of the primer. We have been gratified by the wide range of cooperation we have received from people both in and out of government. Peter Crawford of the OECD set the tone for our Advisory Committee discussions by properly emphasizing the importance of international harmonization. Congressman Bob Eckhardt and members of the staff of the U.S. Environmental Protection Agency—including Steve Jellinek, Marilyn Bracken, and Irving Fuller—willingly gave of their time and effort so that we might grasp the issues more clearly. Martin Uppenbrink and F. Schmidt-Bleek of the Federal Republic of Germany provided assistance in numerous discussions of chemical notification, testing, and control issues. Terry Davies and Bill Reilly of The Conservation Foundation were encouraging and supportive throughout the project. We know also that the project could not have been completed on its tight time schedule without the diligent and careful work of Bob McCoy, who edited the manuscript, and of Tony Brown and Tish Kashani, who typed and retyped the manuscript to meet our sometimes unreasonable deadlines.

Finally, it is our hope that the primer will be significant in two ways. First, we hope that it contributes to informed discussion and decision making by those both in and out of government. Second, we hope that it demonstrates a means by which nongovernment organizations can provide a forum for informal and constructive consideration of national and international issues by different interested parties in ways that are often difficult, if not impossible, to achieve within the more formal confines of official discussions.

Chapter I

Introduction

The products of the chemical industry are everywhere in modern society and are of many kinds: plastics, textiles, construction materials, paints, adhesives, fertilizers, pesticides, and medicines, to name a few. Most chemicals are synthesized from natural gas, petroleum, air, and various ores as basic raw materials, and many depend on sequences of reactions that, during the manufacturing process, create and in turn consume a host of chemicals called intermediates. These intermediates may never reach a broad public but are nonetheless the object of lively trade among specialized companies, often involving transport over long distances.

Some chemicals, like concentrated sulfuric acid and sodium hydroxide, are clearly hazardous and need to be handled in a suitably controlled manner so that the user is protected. The effects of exposure to these chemicals are prompt and obvious. There is no need for sophisticated testing: if a person is injured, he or she knows the source of the injury.

Some chemicals are toxic after repeated exposure at dosage levels too low to create untoward immediate effects. Lead and mercury are classic examples. After exposure at low levels over sometimes long periods, some chemicals produce cancer, birth defects, and harmful genetic and environmental effects.

Some substances, such as benzene and asbestos, can cause cancer,[1] yet appear innocuous at the time of exposure, and give little or no warning of their presence. The onset of the disease may not occur till decades after the exposure. Adverse effects of other chemicals, such as chlorofluorocarbons, may occur after a complex series of processes in the environment which take decades to become fully evident.[2] For cancer and other kinds of delayed health or environmental effects, the connections between the effect, the substance, its manufacturers, and the situation in which the exposure occurred may be difficult or impossible to establish.

Further, no one, including the manufacturer, may know whether a chemical causes long-term (chronic) health effects. In most instances,

1

neither the chemist nor the toxicologist can predict with confidence the toxic properties of a chemical from its chemical structure, boiling or melting points, or other physicochemical data. Even if the immediate (acute) health effects of the chemical have been studied in laboratory animals, the results of these tests usually provide no clue about long-term effects. The state of the art of special studies needed to learn whether cancer or other chronic effects are likely to be caused by a chemical is developing rapidly. However, about 50,000 chemicals are used commercially in the United States;[3] of these, it is estimated that only a few percent have been tested to date for carcinogenesis, sometimes using procedures that do not meet current standards.[4]

Environmental effects, too, are often uncertain since they may depend on complex—sometimes unexpected—interactions and chemical reactions in the environment. To illustrate the complexity that is possible, the adverse effects expected as a consequence of chlorofluorocarbon build-up in the environment are not directly due to the chemicals themselves, but depend on their migration to the upper atmosphere, where they participate in reactions leading to the destruction of naturally occurring ozone. Ozone in the upper atmosphere shields the earth from ultraviolet radiation, which can cause cancer and other adverse effects. Hence, through this indirect route, there is concern that chlorofluorocarbons may lead to unacceptably large increases in the ultraviolet radiation that reaches the earth's surface.[5]

The rate at which testing for health and environmental effects will proceed is tempered by practical limitations of cost and availability of trained scientists and facilities.[6] Yet the need for testing has become increasingly obvious during recent decades, as the chemical industry has grown and as its research has led to a proliferation of new substances.

In setting priorities for future attention, some observers place greatest emphasis on the exposure of workers to chemicals on the job. Some emphasize the sensitivities of groups who may be specially at risk, such as children or women of child-bearing age. Still others point to present and potential effects of chemicals introduced into the natural environment without being readily degraded to harmless materials, particularly when this occurs in large quantities.

The risks caused by these exposures need to be assessed in the light of the benefits derived from the manufacture and use of chemicals. Setting a boundary between acceptable and unacceptable risk is inherently a value judgment. Since risks and benefits can accrue to different groups, such judgments are most appropriately made by persons who can be held publicly accountable for them. Thus, the governments of many countries have been drawn inexorably toward involvement in decisions previously made by chemical manufacturers on their own.

The importance of these matters to legislators, businessmen, and other concerned people can be measured in terms of the risks presented by widespread use of chemicals—often without knowledge of their adverse effects—of the value to society of the industries that manufacture and use chemicals, and of the value of their products.

THE INTENT AND SCOPE OF TOXIC SUBSTANCES CONTROL LAWS

In most countries, legislation to control commercial chemicals has traditionally dealt with occupational exposure and some specific categories of use: pharmaceuticals, foods, food additives, and pesticides. In addition, there is a history of government control of air, water, and drinking-water quality and of land use in relation to disposal of waste products and effluents. Each of these kinds of legislation can be traced to concern about potential or known chemical hazards for which there is extensive environmental distribution, exposure of many people, or repeated exposure of some people over a long period of time.

Only in recent years has it become evident that the security net created by these approaches was incomplete. Seemingly innocuous uses of chemicals were found to cause significant risks. Some have viewed the need for additional legislation to deal with these risks as a filling of gaps in the existing battery of laws, while others have emphasized the need for an internally consistent legislative mechanism for overall control of risks from commercial chemicals. Still others have emphasized development of a comprehensive information system capable of tracing the history of any given commercial chemical from its origin, which would provide the information necessary for careful assessment of risks to human health and the environment.

The earliest U.S. government proposal for toxic substances legislation appeared in April 1971 in the U.S. Council on Environmental Quality report *Toxic Substances.* This report stated:

> Our awareness of environmental threats, our ability to screen and test substances for adverse effects, and our capability to monitor and predict . . . are sufficiently developed that we need no longer remain in a purely reactive posture with respect to toxic substances. We should no longer be limited to repairing the damage after it has been done, nor should we continue to allow the entire population or the entire environment to be used as a laboratory.

A shift in environmental policy toward preventive action, rather than reaction, is also understandable given the nature of the toxic substances that have been in the forefront of public view, namely, carcinogens such as benzene, bis(chloromethyl)ether, vinyl chloride, and asbestos.[7] With widespread use of chemicals, with the expectation that decades may pass between exposure to a chemical and the onset of some adverse effects such as cancer, and with an awareness that most commercial chemicals have been tested incompletely if at all, one can fear that the problem may be very large indeed—and that the optimal time for action may even now be past. On the other hand, the magnitude of the problem may ultimately turn out to be moderate or small. There is even a very real risk that some chemicals which in fact pose a relatively limited and acceptable risk will be incriminated in the public mind. Lacking adequate information on which to base judgments, the room for speculation and differences of viewpoint is immense.

Recognizing that seemingly harmless chemicals may cause injury, legislative initiatives have emphasized testing chemicals and assessing hazard and risk. At the same time, testing is costly, and the need is larger than can now—or even foreseeably—be accommodated by the world corps of trained toxicologists; hence it is necessary to establish a system of priorities by which chemicals are chosen for testing. For example, one strategy embodied in a recent European Community Directive is to focus on only newly marketed chemicals and, for these, to require different degrees of testing for different chemicals, based mainly on their production volumes.

In very general terms, the new generation of legislative initiatives has involved consideration of the following topics:

- development of adequate information on the toxic effects of chemicals on human health and the environment;

- development of sufficient information on the manner and degree to which humans and the environment may be exposed to hazards as a consequence of commerce in these chemicals;

- notification by manufacturers to public officials of information on effects and exposure;

- assessment of risks to human health and the environment;

- control by suitable means of those risks perceived as unacceptable, including packaging and labeling to inform of hazard, as well as restrictions and bans, as appropriate.

THE NEED FOR INTERNATIONAL ACTION

As national policies to control chemicals have been developing, it has become increasingly clear that national measures alone are not sufficient to deal with some of the major issues, since there are problems that cannot be resolved solely within a national context. Three essentially independent factors contribute to this situation.

First, international trade in chemicals is of vital importance to the economic well-being of many countries. Chemical trade among OECD members alone was over $90 billion in 1975. This can be compared to chemical sales in OECD countries of $300 billion in 1977, and total employment in the chemical industry of just under 4 million people.[8] The chemical industry is dependent on access to world markets. Noncompatible systems of control, with their potential for duplicative and conflicting requirements, might restrict trade.

Second, substances cross national boundaries in many kinds of manufactured articles such as television sets and autos. An importer can hardly be required to obtain information on all of the many chemicals, possibly originating in several countries, that can be present as part of a complex article such as a tractor or a suit of clothes. Domestic authorities consequently will likely find themselves in a position where they will need to depend to some degree on the existence of compatible control systems in other countries. If only one nation that exports products does not have a system of control that is compatible with the rest, a loophole may be created through which chemicals of unknown identity can pass.

Third, it is impossible to limit the environmental effects of chemicals to a single country; substances can be transported from one country to another through the air, through water, or through food chains. The most dramatic example of this ecological linkage is the presence of DDT in birds at the polar ice cap, hundreds, perhaps even thousands, of miles away from any application of the pesticide.[9] Moreover, certain effects occur outside national jurisdictions but may constitute a threat to many or all nations, such as accumulation of mercury in fish or interactions with chlorofluorocarbons in the ozone layer of the upper atmosphere.

Internationally compatible control strategies are generally desirable in dealing with environmental and health problems having international implications. But for toxic substances there are also compelling economic, trade, and administrative reasons to make all concerned—government, industry, the interested public—seek international solutions. Indeed, it is difficult to see how a practical approach to control of chemicals can evolve without an active effort by countries to achieve internationally compatible goals.

THE STRUCTURE OF THE INTERNATIONAL SYSTEM

The development of an international system of health and environmental protection is based on an intricate interplay between national and international considerations. The activities of international organizations are, in effect, a highly developed form of information exchange aimed at achieving compatible national policies. The primary audiences are the governments of the member states of the organizations involved, largely because nations and their governments are the principal actors in any noncommercial form of international cooperation. To achieve results that are binding on the nations concerned, ultimately the only available vehicle is the signing and ratification of an international convention, which can be either bilateral or multilateral. Such conventions consequently make up the backbone of the entire international system for the management of environmental and health problems.

Much negotiation is required before and after the signing of a convention. An international treaty obligation takes precedence over prior national law; thus, international negotiation can have serious ramifications for subsequent national practice. In some circumstances, national policy decisions may, in effect, be made at an international level. Hence, it is vital that the issues being considered in international discusssions be understood fully by all groups in all nations concerned with toxic substances control at any level.

The European Community (EC)

The European Community (EC) is a regional institution with legislative power. It derives this power from the Treaty of Rome, agreed to by the Member States: Belgium, Denmark, France, the Federal Republic of Germany, Ireland, Italy, Luxembourg, The Netherlands, and the United Kingdom. The Member States will include Greece as of 1981, not long thereafter Spain, and, ultimately, Portugal. The EC has the ability to adopt, among other instruments, directives that define procedures and objectives. The Member States are bound by the Treaty of Rome to take all necessary measures to assure that these procedures and objectives are fully incorporated into their national laws within a period of time specified in each directive. They can exercise individual discretion in the measures required to achieve this in the context of their respective legal systems, but the EC institutions have a right to review the results. The EC can take steps, if necessary, to assure compliance through a judgment of the European Court of Justice, an independent institution of the Community. Thus, EC directives have the effect of achieving compatible results by defining the criteria of compatibility but not the specific means by which the Member States will achieve this result.

The recently enacted EC Directive of 18 September 1979 (79/831/EEC) "amending for the sixth time Directive 67/548/EEC on the approximation of the laws, regulations and administrative provisions relating to the classification, packaging and labelling of dangerous substances" will lead to the development of compatible systems for testing and notification to governments of chemicals placed on the market, as well as requirements for classification, packaging, and labeling of dangerous substances in the Member States. It is certainly important to recognize the Directive (79/831/EEC) for what it is. Although it is not a national law, it will lead directly to national laws in accordance with the Directive in nine and, ultimately, in twelve countries of Europe. Compliance with 79/831/EEC requires that implementation by the Member States shall occur by September 18, 1981, and may include additional elements not covered by 79/831/EEC. But, in those areas defined by the Directive, the Member States have no discretion as to the results. As a consequence, its effects are quite predictable.

Since the EC can legislate, it has assured that an international system of compatible toxic substances control policies will come into being among its Member States. Linkages with countries outside the Community will be more difficult procedurally, given that no legislative mechanisms exist. Such agreements will ultimately need to be negotiated by traditional diplomatic procedures.

Organisation for Economic Cooperation and Development (OECD)

The Organisation for Economic Cooperation and Development (OECD) is an international organization set up under a convention signed in Paris in 1960, and based on the premises that:

- a high degree of international economic interdependence is beneficial for economic growth and social progress;

- intergovernmental cooperation among like-minded, market-economy industrialized countries can help to solve the problems they are facing together as well as those that confront them in their relations with each other and the outside world.

Twenty-four countries are members of the OECD, including the nine member countries of the EC, plus Australia, Austria, Canada, Finland, Greece, Iceland, Japan, New Zealand, Norway, Portugal, Spain, Sweden, Switzerland, Turkey, and the United States. Yugoslavia is a "special status" country—it participates in many of the OECD activities without having the right to vote. Provision has also been made for the Commission of the EC to take part in the work of the Organisation, and it is represented in many of the OECD bodies.

The governing body of the OECD is the Council, composed of permanent representatives from all member countries.

While the OECD is quite different from the EC in its scope, as it has no authority to legislate, there are several courses of action available to the Council to achieve international agreements and understandings. These include:

- Council Recommendations: A recommendation is not legally binding, but it carries with it a strong moral obligation. Usually a recommendation is accompanied by follow-up procedures, that is, procedures whereby countries report on steps taken to implement the recommendation.

- Council Decisions: Except as otherwise provided, a decision is binding on governments.

- International Treaties or Agreements: Member governments may, within the framework of OECD, negotiate an international treaty or agreement. Normally, the text of the agreement is set first in a council decision and the formal agreement is later signed by governments. Such treaties are then subject to normal national ratification procedures.

The OECD has shown its ability to develop rapidly programs dealing with policy related to its primary economic missions—ranging from education and employment through environmental protection to energy—and to provide information useful for members.

Member States of the OECD account for a very large part of the world production of chemicals, a similarly large part of world trade, and for almost all new commercially produced chemicals.[10] Thus, the OECD has a natural interest in issues of chemical control.

The OECD has pursued a broad-ranging chemicals program. The main purpose of this program has been to harmonize regulatory approaches to:

- facilitate concerted action on common problems;
- reduce nontariff barriers to trade;
- reduce the cost burden associated with testing;
- effectively use available resources.

The present OECD chemicals program focuses on three key areas for international harmonization—namely, testing, information exchange, and evaluation of information in the context of assessing and controlling chemical risks.

General Agreement on Tariff and Trade (GATT)

The General Agreement on Tariff and Trade (GATT), the title of a treaty, is also the name of the secretariat that is responsible for the treaty's administration and updating. The object of the GATT is to encourage free trade. It recognizes that certain practices can lead to nontariff trade barriers. Among those practices, insofar as chemicals are concerned, can be inequities in the nature of test requirements, or the standards for accepting or interpreting the results of these tests. There is a mechanism for redress through the GATT if one member nation claims that the conduct of another nation creates an inequity. There is also an escape clause by which national health, safety, and environmental protection can be a sufficient basis for rebuttal of such claims.

The conditions and procedures by which appeals to GATT on chemical control issues can be initiated, as well as the manner in which they will be handled, can only be described in general terms at this time. There are many new questions. Thus, while it is premature to present any judgments of the role that GATT will play during the years ahead in toxic substances control, it could be an important factor in the future. The practices that may be considered barriers to trade are discussed in greater detail in Chapter VI.

Other International Organizations

A number of other international organizations are already playing important roles in developing, assessing, and transferring information on chemicals. The World Health Organisation (WHO), for example, publishes documents that establish environmental health criteria for chemical substances. WHO has also long worked with the Food and Agriculture Organisation (FAO) in a Food Standards Program which develops standards for food additives and pesticide residues. The International Labor Organisation (ILO) keeps track of chemical hazards to workers. The United Nations Environment Programme (UNEP) is a coordinating and initiating body with limited financing capacity; it is responsible for the International Register of Potentially Toxic Chemicals (IRPTC), which may be particularly important in informing developing countries about chemical hazards. As of January 1980, IRPTC had national correspondents in 68 countries. UNEP and ILO are cooperating in an International Occupational Safety and Health Hazard Alert System, with UNEP concentrating on the environment as a whole, and ILO on the work environment.[11]

The World Health Assembly of WHO has initiated an International Programme on Chemical Safety. ILO and UNEP have agreed to work closely with WHO in this program, and FAO also will probably be involved. The program's proposed activities include: developing methodologies for testing and risk assessment, selecting priority chemicals for evaluation of health and environmental effects, collecting and disseminating information, helping improve response to chemical accidents, and developing manpower training programs.[12]

The International Agency for Research on Cancer (IARC) is an independent body within WHO. It prepares critical reviews of data on the risk of cancer from chemicals to which humans may be exposed.

Organizations such as the Council of Europe have been involved at the regional level. The Council has played a part in an effort to harmonize pharmaceutical terminology.

THE U.S. TOXIC SUBSTANCES CONTROL ACT, THE EUROPEAN COMMUNITY DIRECTIVE, AND OTHER TOXIC SUBSTANCES CONTROL LAWS

The U.S. Toxic Substances Control Act (TSCA) and the European Community Directive 79/831/EEC define many of the salient procedures and standards by which toxic characteristics of chemicals are to be identified and controlled. Each of these legislative acts is binding on major producers of chemical substances. Moreover, the character of 79/831/EEC as a legislative act representative of the collective will of nine countries means that it must be accorded particular weight from any international perspective.

The EC and the United States account for a large proportion of world chemical exports.[13] In 1979, for example, the value of total world chemical exports was $122.5 billion. The nine EC members accounted for $68 billion, over half the total; the United States accounted for another $17.3 billion. Thus, neither 79/831/EEC nor TSCA can rationally be set aside in any discussion of emerging world patterns of chemical control, though emphasis on them in no way minimizes or denies the importance of other national and international initiatives. In their similarities and differences, TSCA and 79/831/EEC can be claimed to define most of the major issues that need to be addressed, for at least some years to come.

For these reasons, it is tempting to seek definitive understanding of TSCA and the EC Directive. By a comparative study one might then hope to master their implications for the chemical industry, for trade in chemical products, as well as for health and environmental protection. This might be an achievable goal if the consequences of both pieces of legislation were clear in all their details. For different reasons and in different ways, as discussed in Chapter II, this is not now the case.

Perhaps it is better that much remains to be made explicit. Though TSCA and the 79/831/EEC are similar in many important ways, they differ in scope of coverage, in requirements, and perhaps even in goals. Most of these differences may be reconcilable, many obviously will be. The two approaches may be made more or less compatible, depending on the mutual accommodations that are made during their implementation. Also, any piece of legislation can be amended for compelling reasons. As these matters are elaborated in increasing detail during the coming months and years, it will, however, become ever more difficult for a boldly new approach to emerge that does not fit into the context of the ongoing debate on TSCA and the national implementations, by the EC Member States, of 79/831/EEC.

In much of the remainder of this primer, TSCA and 79/831/EEC will be used to create a context for discussion of key issues. Though such focus on TSCA and 79/831/EEC is in part a device to illustrate and describe key substantive issues, it is also an acknowledgement that these pieces of legislation are at the center of the world stage—and command particular attention.

The U.S. Toxic Substances Control Act

Prior to the enactment of TSCA, U.S. regulatory authority did not extend to all commercial chemicals or to all uses of chemicals, and generally did not authorize direct controls at an early stage of commercial development. For example, although the Food and Drug Administration and the Consumer Product Safety Commission could regulate certain uses of chlorofluoro-carbons, other uses could not be regulated.

Moreover, while some authority existed to control the production of specific categories of substances, such as pesticides,[14] food additives and drugs,[15] and fuel additives,[16] most U.S. statutes did not authorize regulatory mechanisms for direct control of commercial chemical products. For example, the Clean Air Act and the Clean Water Act, both amended in 1977, focus on toxic pollutants at the point at which they are released to the environment either in the form of discharges to water or emissions to the air. They do not control chemicals in manufactured products. The Occupational Safety and Health Act (1970) authorizes the promulgation of health and safety standards for the protection of workers, but it does not authorize regulation of the uses of particular chemical substances.

In its first approach to toxic substances control legislation in 1971, the Senate used the model of older acts dealing with drugs, and animal, insect, and plant poisons.[17] The Senate bill envisaged something in the nature of premarket screening of chemicals before they were to be permitted to come on the market. In contrast, the House approach[18] was that of notification, identification by the Environmental Protection Agency of dangerous chemicals, and selection of certain chemicals for testing.

A House-Senate conference committee met for more than a year without producing any legislative product. The Senate conferees objected to the weakness of the notification provisions in the House bill, and the House conferees objected to the Senate bill's restrictive screening provisions, which were felt to impair innovation in chemical development.[19] The entire 93rd Congress and most of the 94th afforded a kind of incubation period for the final draft of the Toxic Substances Control Act.

The salient characteristic of TSCA, as it finally emerged in 1976, was that of notification for new chemicals. The manufacturer or importer must give notice to EPA 90 days in advance of commercial manufacture or importation. Such notice must include information concerning the structure, uses, and proposed volume of production of the new chemical. The manufacturer or importer must report what he knows and can reasonably find out about the health and environmental effects of the chemical.

The law authorizes EPA to prohibit or limit manufacture of those new chemicals determined to be unreasonably dangerous on the basis of all available information, including the testing that has been conducted. EPA is also authorized to delay the manufacture or importation of chemicals that may be dangerous but have not been adequately tested; this restriction is available pending the development of additional information. However, if the manufacturer or importer files its disagreement with EPA's conclusions, then the chemical can flow to commercial usage unless EPA enjoins the manufacturer or importer in court.

Of course, before the Act's provisions could apply to new chemicals intended to enter commerce, it was necessary to determine first what is old—that is, already in commerce. This is dealt with in TSCA by listing on an inventory chemicals presently used for commercial purposes. Then, what is new is determined by exception, that is, a chemical is new if it is not on the inventory. As each new chemical is manufactured, TSCA provides for its addition to the inventory, so that each new chemical is notified only by its first manufacturer or importer. Under TSCA, new chemicals, in effect, become old chemicals after they are first manufactured or imported.

TSCA describes procedures and standards by which EPA may require testing of particular chemicals or categories of chemicals, new and old, by manufacturers or importers. It creates authority and sets standards by which EPA may control chemicals by any of a wide variety of options— labeling, for example, or restrictions and bans on production or use.

The principal goal of TSCA is to prevent unreasonable risk of injury to health and the environment due to commercial chemicals. Notification, testing, information gathering, and control are all parts of a complex procedural web by which unreasonable risks may be identified and suitably controlled.

The EC Directive (79/831/EEC)

A similar emphasis on control was also evident early during the EC deliberations that ultimately led to passage of 79/831/EEC. When the EC Council adopted the Action Programme for the Environment in November 1973, it specifically charged the Commission "to investigate the measures still required to harmonize and strengthen *control* by public authorities over chemicals before they are marketed" (emphasis added). Between June 1975 and September 1976, the Commission met with a group of experts who came from all nine Community countries to try to work out the details of the approach that might be followed at the Community level.

At the time the Commission began its work, there already existed a Council Directive known as 67/548/EEC. This Directive, adopted originally in 1967 and subsequently amended several times, dealt with the classification, packaging, and labeling of dangerous substances. The Directive established various categories of dangerous substances, such as explosive, flammable, corrosive, irritant, and so on; it imposed an obligation on the Member States of the Community to classify dangerous substances according to the nature of the hazard and to ensure that such substances would not be put on the market unless they were packaged and labeled according to the provisions of the Directive.

Specifically, the 1967 Directive required that every package of a dangerous substance must show clearly and indelibly:

- the name of the substance;

- the origin of the substance;

- the danger symbol, where this has been designated, and an indication of the danger involved in the use of the substance;

- a reference to special risks; and

- safety advice.

The Directive provided a list of standard phrases for indicating special risks and also some standard wording for safety advice. The Directive also provided for establishment of a Community list of substances that have been classified as dangerous under the Directive. As of mid-1980, over 800 substances had been thus classified.[20]

After much consideration and many meetings with the experts of the Member States, the Commission decided that the 1967 Directive was an appropriate vehicle to handle the question of the notification of new chemical substances that could, in the sense already described, be considered "dangerous" for the environment. In September 1976, the Commission sent a proposal to the Council for a sixth modification of the 1967 Directive. This proposal expanded the principles of the 1967 Directive so as to cover not only the classification, packaging, and labeling of dangerous substances but also notification of newly marketed substances. In accordance with the Community's legislative procedure, the proposal was sent to the European Parliament and to the Economic and Social Committee (composed of representatives of employers, employees, and other social and professional groups). Both bodies reviewed and endorsed the proposal, with some suggestions for modifications.

After three years of negotiation, the Council of the Community approved Directive 79/831/EEC on September 18, 1979, a substantially modified version of the 1976 proposal. It is to be implemented by Member States within two years of the date of approval—that is, by September 18, 1981.

As under TSCA, an inventory of substances (in this case, those on the Community market as of September 18, 1981) is to be prepared, but, in contrast to TSCA, new substances do not upon notification become inscribed on the inventory. They remain "new," so that each subsequent manufacturer or importer must also prepare and submit a notification. Notification must be given before substances are placed on the market, which contrasts with notification in TSCA before manufacture or importation. These differences of notification between TSCA and 79/831/EEC, discussed in greater detail in Chapter IV, lead to important differences in who must notify and what chemicals require notification.

The 79/831/EEC Directive is more specific than TSCA in stating the health, environmental, and physicochemical test data that must accompany a new chemical notification. The EC Directive does not, however, contain provisions for testing old substances. Further, in contrast to TSCA, the Directive is concerned with only a limited number of the many possible control measures for dealing with health and environmental risks. It covers testing requirements, definitions (based on the results of these tests) for determining whether substances are to be considered dangerous, and an injunction against the marketing of dangerous substances unless they are packaged and labeled in prescribed ways. Stated differently, if testing, notification, packaging, and labeling are in accord with the Directive, there is no obstacle in Community law to chemicals being placed on the market. As already noted, this contrasts with TSCA, which presents a host of options for limiting, delaying, or preventing manufacture or marketing.

It is essential to emphasize that TSCA is a national law, while 79/831/EEC is a Directive addressed to the nations that comprise the European Community. To comply with the Directive, each EC Member State will need to bring its national law into conformity with the Directive's provisions by September 1981. In many instances, this will require the enactment of new laws. EC Member States, in their national laws, may include provisions that deal with issues outside the scope of 79/831/EEC, such as testing of old chemicals. (The Community, too, is not precluded from dealing with additional aspects of chemical control at some future date, and, should that occur, Member States will need to conform with any additional Community requirements.)

The different contexts of national laws in the United States and legislative initiatives in Europe are described in Chapter II. These must be understood to appreciate how differences between TSCA and 79/831/EEC may be dealt with most constructively.

Other National Chemical Control Laws

At least eight other countries have laws that provide some authority to regulate new chemicals. Many of these laws also apply to existing substances. The laws generally permit regulation of production, import, sale, and use. Some also govern areas such as labeling and disposal.

In 1969, Switzerland became the first country to have a general chemical control law. Its Law on Trade in Toxic Substances requires notification be given for all chemical substances and products before they are marketed. They are then classified in one of five groups on the basis of their acute toxicity. Conditions of sale and use are set for each category.

Sweden has both a 1973 Act on Products Hazardous to Man or the Environment and a 1979 Ordinance on Product Notification. A producer or importer of a substance that is either new or listed must examine the substance for hazardous effects on humans and the environment; the producer or importer must make all information on the chemical available on request to the government. Special permission may be required to produce a substance or product if it is considered dangerous. Substances may also be banned. The 1979 Ordinance requires the producer or importer to identify the chemical composition of products, including impurities, that would be significant in evaluating health and environmental hazards.

Japan's 1973 Chemical Substances Control Act considers a chemical new if it is not among the approximately 19,000 substances on a list compiled in 1973. A manufacturer or importer must inform the government about a new substance. Tests on persistence, accumulation, and toxicity to humans are then performed at the expense of the manufacturer. A substance is classified as a dangerous substance or a safe substance. While the chemical is being classified, a manufacturer or importer may start production or importation, but must register such actions.

The United Kingdom's Control of Pollution Act of 1974 allows the government to restrict production, import, sale, or use of a chemical substance.

Canada's Environmental Contaminants Act of 1975 classifies a new substance as one that is manufactured or imported for the first time in amounts of more than 500 kg. per year. All information on effects must be submitted to the government within three months of manufacture or import. The government may also require tests to be carried out. A substance may be placed on a list of dangerous substances and measures taken to limit or ban its use.

Norway's Product Control Act of 1976 is generally similar to Sweden's law.

France's Chemicals Control Act of 1977 requires producers and importers of new chemicals and chemicals for new uses to provide information needed to determine their effects on people and the environment. Marketing is permitted 30 days after the information is provided. The dossier may be accepted, or further testing may be required. The substance may be banned or its use limited.

In Denmark, the Chemical Substances and Products Act of 1979 provides for notification. A new substance is one placed on the market after October 1, 1980. Any substance used for a significantly altered purpose or in significantly increased quantities after that date must also be notified. The government may restrict or ban the sale, import, or use of a substance to ensure that it does not present any hazards to health or the environment.

Austria, Australia, the Federal Republic of Germany, and The Netherlands are among the nations preparing new legislation on chemical notification, testing, and control. Switzerland is considering amending its earlier legislation.

Chapter II

Context

When seeking to understand national laws concerning toxic substances, it is essential to consider the language of the laws and regulations in the context of each nation's legal, political, and social institutions and traditions. Key aspects of a law's application are embedded in unwritten assumptions about the relationships between branches of the national government, between levels of government, or between government and private associations and individuals. These considerations become still more important if one seeks to understand the processes of lawmaking in the European Community (EC), which must do its work in a manner consistent with different political cultures, with the Roman law traditions of the Continent, and with the common law traditions of the United Kingdom and Ireland.

Perhaps the best illustration of this complexity is the way in which the EC handles terminological problems, arising from the existence of six official languages. In effect, the EC is "sovereign" in its use of the six languages. It does not, for example, require the approval of the Danish government to assign a legal meaning to a Danish word. Thus, legal terms in English, or in the other Community languages for that matter, can have quite different meanings as used by the EC from what they have in national laws. While the Community, of course, seeks to avoid such a situation, this is not always possible.

THE NATIONAL CONTEXT:
LEGAL, POLITICAL, AND SOCIAL FACTORS

Differences in tradition, law, and outlook have already affected the development of toxic substances policies in the major industrial countries, and will also affect the process of international communication and adaptation of these policies in the future.

The Creation of Laws

The U.S. Congress, through its system of committees with extensive and trained staff, plays a public and important role in the creation of laws. In contrast to normal European parliamentary practice, many U.S. national laws originate in the Congress or are substantially changed after submission to the Congress by the Executive. As members of Congress develop expertise and seniority, their personal views on particular policies may find considerable reflection in the final shape of the law. Toxic substances control bills, differing in important particulars, were carefully shepherded through House and Senate committee hearings and debates by Congressman Bob Eckhardt and Senator John Tunney.

In European countries, fundamental decisions about the structure and reach of a national law are made at a relatively secret preparliamentary drafting stage except in very rare cases. During the drafting state, there is an extensive process of review by political parties represented in the national legislatures and by leading national private organizations. This occurs before the drafts are made public, rather than during the period of public consideration by the legislature. The specific play of forces varies, of course, from one country to another.

In several countries, and in the EC itself, there are consultative bodies with considerable constitutional prerogatives; they are generally called "economic and social committees." Their function is to ensure that various social groups—employers, trade unions, professional groups, farmers, small businesses, consumers—are heard when laws are being formulated. Thus far, environmental groups only rarely have been given a voice in these bodies.

Where such bodies do not exist, other mechanisms are employed for consensus-building: Royal Commissions in the United Kingdom; Special Commissions in Sweden or Norway; and permanent independent expert commissions and formalized consultations between employers and trade unions in Germany. In many instances, political parties have long-standing and sometimes even formalized relationships with such groups as trade unions or small business, leading representatives of which may also be members of parliaments. Therefore, the parties tend to represent a supplementary conduit for input into legislation before it emerges into public discussion.

The executive branches of national European governments are voted into office (or can at the very least be removed from office) by a majority in parliament. In several countries, ministers are required to be members of parliament. In most countries of western Europe, a prime task of the government of the day is to maintain a working majority in parliament, since the government's very existence depends on this majority. Thus, the executive branches of European governments are particularly sensitive to the views of the political parties controlling parliaments.

The result, as mentioned above, is that in Europe the suggestions of the representatives of most interest groups and of various political party factions are often already reflected in draft laws when they are submitted to the national parliament. The ensuing parliamentary hearings and debates often focus on specific issues or differences of opinion that could not be reconciled at the earlier stage.

One result of this practice is to increase the weight of the political party organizations in the processes of legislation. A second result is to protect government deliberations from mass campaigns and relatively new pressure groups or citizen organizations. The European governments favor this relatively closed process. They believe it leads to the creation of objective laws; it appears to them to be much more orderly than the seemingly wide-open American process. On the other hand, Americans may tend to believe that the European process limits the lawmaking function of the national legislatures and does not provide a sufficiently broadly based democratic process for citizen participation.

European laws are considered much less subject to later amendment than American laws. The U.S. Congress is often more willing to experiment with new approaches, and then to review the law after a period of time to make necessary, possibly fundamental, adjustments. Such is the faith of some European countries in their executive governments that some laws merely authorize the Executive to prepare regulations that will achieve certain general goals. The U.S. Congress may enact laws that are similarly unstructured and general, but differences in administrative process in Europe compared to the United States mean that the seemingly equivalent degree of generality has vastly different impacts on administrative implementation.

Creation of Regulations

The process of administrative rule making in the United States is open to the public. The law specifically defines extensive opportunities for public participation. The process also requires public, formal justification of the chosen administrative rule. The rule-making process triggered in a statute like TSCA by the words "if the Administrator finds that . . . ," may take months or years to complete. The requirement that each regulatory control action regarding a specific chemical or category of chemicals take the form of an administrative rule places a heavy burden on the U.S. Environmental Protection Agency to choose its regulatory actions carefully.

The verb *find* is heavily weighted with meaning from the U.S. Administrative Procedure Act,[1] which requires that a rule be based on written findings, which are a series of statements of fact indicating that the situation justifies the regulatory action; the relationship between the rule and the findings is subject to judicial review.

The U.S. Freedom of Information Act[2] strengthens the public character of the regulatory process in the United States by requiring that most documents in the possession of the government be available to the public. Public documents can include records of all contacts between the responsible government official and people interested in a proposed regulation—publication of the official's conversations with private persons, even schedules of appointments.

In contrast, the normal European practice is to prepare regulations by circulating proposals to selected representatives of important societal groups (including labor, industry, local governments, noted scholars, church officials, and the political parties) in comparative secrecy and without direct involvement of the public.

These differences in the process of creating regulations mean that European regulations undergo a relatively quiet process of consensus building before they become public, while American regulations emerge from a series of public, controversial discussions.

Europeans often fear that American administrators have too much discretion and may establish overly restrictive regulations. This fear is based on a lack of awareness of the unstated U.S. procedural and political restraints on the development of administrative policy. Americans, on the other hand, may assume that the closed consensus approach toward creating regulations in Europe means that important, nonquantifiable environmental considerations will be overpowered by traditional, powerful economic interests because individuals and newer, public interest organizations, such as environmental and urban groups, are seldom invited to share in the consultation process.

In many European countries a concept of similar importance to the U.S. rule-making process is the principle that regulations must be unambiguous so as to protect the citizen from arbitrary state action. The importance of this principle rests on the greater relative power of European States over their citizens, and a much weaker system of checks and balances in many countries. This standard of legal certitude has posed serious difficulties in dealing with environmental problems, where the rationale for a decision may cease to be valid when new and different facts become available or when circumstances change the patterns of use or exposure to a chemical.

Once taken, administrative decisions in many Continental European countries can be difficult to change.

Judicial Review

Environmental regulations in the United States have been particularly prone to challenge in court. Since court proceedings can take a long time and are expensive, some observers believe that administrative agencies find it prudent to create regulations that leave little room for challenge in court—that is, regulations that are conservative enough to discourage attack.

European courts accord the decisions of administrators much greater deference. The traditional respect accorded the professional civil servant may, in part, explain why judicial review in Europe seldom extends to examination of the basic validity of a national or state regulation. Scrutiny by the courts can also be limited by doctrines protecting the "sphere of decision making" of the administration from judicial review, with only a few exceptions such as extreme cases of arbitrariness.

The administrative courts in the Federal Republic of Germany, however, seem to be moving toward more substantive judicial review. Rising public protests about the power of the bureaucracy in Germany have led jurists to give more attention to review of administrative decisions, thus opening the courts for consideration of many specific issues not previously considered judicially reviewable. This opportunity has been used by industry and environmental groups alike. Nonetheless, the courts in the Federal Republic of Germany, as well as elsewhere in Europe, play a much smaller role in the decision-making process leading to environmental control than is the case in the United States.

Federalism and Central Governments

The implementation of laws and regulations is greatly affected by the distribution of administrative and legislative authority among the parts of a central national government, or the various levels of government. Countries with a federalist structure, such as the United States, the Federal Republic of Germany, or Italy, must cope with a degree of decentralized decision making and implementation of national policies that is unimaginable in a state with a strong central government, such as France.

There is understandably some concern in international discussions that the laws and regulations of national governments with a federalist structure may be preempted by other levels of government. This issue is addressed explicitly by TSCA in a manner that limits the authority of U.S. States, and political subdivisions of States, where EPA has imposed requirements under TSCA.

Cooperation

Regulatory traditions may also play a large role in the implementation of laws and regulations. A century-old European tradition of industrial controls exists, for example, in France, The Netherlands, Great Britain, Germany, and Sweden; this leads to considerable involvement of the regulatory agency in the life of industry, but may also mean that controls are less strict in specific instances, since a relationship of trust has been built up over the years between the local agency office and the industry. That relationship may hold true whether the local office represents a state or a national authority.

A U.S. regulatory agency, such as the U.S. Environmental Protection Agency, cannot rely on a tradition of shared trust and mutual confidence in dealings with industry. Instead, the traditional relationship is adversarial. As new laws and regulations take force, decisions that were previously left up to industry—especially general environmental, health, and safety decisions—are removed to the authority of an agency in which the industry may have little confidence. This continuing source of tension in the United States may help mystified Europeans understand why the American environmental regulatory process appears to move in fits and starts, with sometimes bitter public controversies finally decided by the courts.

INTERNATIONAL LINKAGES

In the foregoing section, we have advanced some fairly far-reaching generalizations about "Europe" and the United States. But "Europe," however defined, is itself comprised of nations with widely differing traditions. There are several groupings of Western European states. These range from the Economic Commission for Europe (a UN body that also includes Canada and the United States) to the Nordic Council and the Benelux countries. Only the Council of Europe or the European Community (EC), however, provide the justification for speaking about "Europe" in a collective sense.

The Council of Europe comprises all parliamentary democracies in Europe and is tied together by the European Convention on Human Rights, a document roughly corresponding in its scope to the American Bill of Rights. The European Community, on the other hand, is the only multilateral body that has systematic experience with the complex problem of how to achieve comparable results through uniform legislation applied in widely differing legal systems. Of equal importance, it is concerned with how to avoid having unilateral national legislation lead to the creation of obstacles to the free movement of people and goods. The result is a highly complex network of relationships among national legislation, Community legislation, and national action. Even most Europeans have not yet learned to deal regularly or effectively with this unique new situation.

As a rule, Community legislation cannot pass the EC Council of Ministers without a unanimous vote of the Ministers, representing all Member States. In practice, Community actions tend to conform with, rather than diverge from, present laws in Member States, since no government could accept Community legislation in blatant contradiction of a law that had previously been voted by its own national parliament. In many instances, notably in the field of chemicals legislation, Community action was closely linked to a national initiative—in this instance, French legislation.

The French law defined the frame of reference for the Community and, in turn, enactment of Directive 79/831/EEC can be expected to trigger revisions in the French law. A party to the unanimous adoption of this Directive by the Community, France has, in effect, made a commitment to revise its law as needed to conform with the Directive.

Once a country moves to implement Community decisions, its entire policymaking structure is mobilized. However, since not every participant in the subsequent national debate will be aware of the full impact of prior EC decisions on the national action that follows, it sometimes proves quite difficult to achieve the required results in national bodies.

Only slowly are Europeans in the Community learning to play the EC level with or against the national level. In some instances, it may prove easier to obtain desired results by a "detour" via Community legislation than by direct national action, because of constitutional or political constraints in the national situation. In the specific area of chemical control, it is likely that several states would have adopted no legislation or much less stringent legislation without Community pressures.[3]

Beyond these linkages among European nations, there is, of course, a strong sense of linkage between Europe and the United States because of historical ties, because of significant international trade, and also because of the many treaties and other agreements, both formal and informal, that connect the two. Indeed, both are also linked to still other areas of the world through OECD, the United Nations, and other mechanisms. No comprehensive analysis of such linkages is possible within the context of this limited discussion, though it is important to acknowledge that such connections do exist and are important.

LIMITED RESOURCES AND SETTING PRIORITIES

The large number of chemicals, and the cost of collecting and analyzing information about their possible effects, makes it essential to set priorities for testing and regulation. For example, the current U.S. TSCA inventory lists the approximately 50,000 chemical substances now being manufactured or imported into the United States. Estimates of the number of new substances that will be added each year range between 400 and 1,000. To perform fairly complete testing of a substance for a broad range of toxic effects, including birth defects, genetic effects, cancer, behavioral effects, and environmental effects, is very expensive and takes many years. Shortages of trained personnel and of some types of facilities already exist. A regulatory decision to control a chemical is also time consuming and expensive, for government and industry alike, requiring extensive collection and analysis of economic as well as scientific information. Thus, limitations of funds and trained personnel, coupled with the large number of substances that might be studied, lead inescapably to the need to choose some substances that will receive greater priority than others.

There is an incentive to avoid costly duplication of testing in different countries. Moreover, countries with little or no production of new chemicals are also less likely to have the capacity to test old chemicals or to evaluate information about imported chemicals. Thus, setting testing priorities has international consequences, even when nations unilaterally select their own priorities for testing.

In its focus on new substances, 79/831/EEC, in effect, makes a major decision about priorities: particular attention will be directed primarily to new chemicals. The volume of production for the chemical is the major criterion by which additional consideration of testing, beyond a base set of tests, is required. This "step sequence" (hierarchical) approach sets priorities for testing beyond the base set.

The United States under TSCA has not as yet developed as highly articulated a plan as the EC to set priorities for testing of new chemicals, though EPA has expressed its intent to establish testing guidelines. EPA is exploring a screening mechanism that groups new chemical notifications into high-, medium-, and low-risk categories for purposes of administrative processing. As yet, however, there are no specific criteria for determining whether more information about a new chemical should be required or what information should be developed. As a first step, however, EPA now plans to adopt as guidance the minimum pre-market data set (MPD) developed by the OECD. EPA is also participating in the OECD's continuing work to develop a hierarchical approach to testing.

The amount of consideration a notice gets in the United States is, in practice, partially determined by the number of notices submitted during a particular period of time, since EPA has a maximum of 180 days to evaluate a notice and only limited resources to devote to review. However, there are later opportunities under TSCA, after the notification period expires, for

EPA to again evaluate a substance and decide whether additional testing is needed.

For old chemicals, the EC has not yet issued any directive concerning systematic screening for toxic hazards. In the absence of a Community mandate, national laws may set priorities for old chemicals, and national administrations can exercise a certain amount of discretion. Denmark, to take one example, has decided to devote a significant proportion of its testing resources to old chemicals.

In the United States, TSCA does provide a means to set priorities for testing old chemicals. An Interagency Testing Committee (ITC), established by TSCA, recommends substances to EPA for priority consideration. The recommendations are in the form of a list of substances, not to exceed 50 substances at any time. The list may be revised by the Committee periodically. (The Committee is comprised of representatives from many U.S. federal agencies.) The method of selecting chemicals has been a scoring system for degree of human and environmental exposure and what can reasonably be expected about toxic effects.[4] The Committee is required to consider, where relevant, the amount of a chemical produced annually, the amount entering the environment, the number of individuals exposed at work and the duration of their exposure, the extent of human exposure, whether the substance is closely related to others known to present unreasonable risk, data presently available on health and environmental effects, whether testing will yield information useful for prediction of effects, and whether facilities and personnel for testing are available. Seven types of effects have been considered by ITC: cancer, genetic effects, birth defects, acute toxicity, other toxicity, bioaccumulation, and ecological effects. The ITC scoring system is not fixed, and can be expected to change on the basis of ongoing experience.

EPA also has authority under TSCA to establish a list of substances that present or may present an unreasonable risk. This provision has not yet been used.

In the long run, perhaps the most important means that TSCA provides for setting priorities is the authority to apply requirements to categories of substances instead of individual substances. So far this authority has been used in only a few instances. Many different kinds of categories might be used. They might relate, for example, to chemical structure, production volume, use, type of toxic effect, effects on specified sensitive populations, or the number of individuals exposed. TSCA provides wide latitude in the criteria by which categories may be defined, but specifically does not permit substances to be grouped in a category solely because they are new substances. Categories of substances may be used in handling premanufacture notifications, or in any other kind of action under TSCA.

Whether or how to use categories has been intensively debated in the United States. Some have argued that the number of chemicals in commerce, and the amount of information needed, makes the use of categories a practical necessity for both testing and regulating chemicals. Others have argued that the unique toxicological characteristics of each chemical make it inappropriate to use categories, or at least inappropriate to use them widely. There are many as yet unanswered legal, scientific, economic, social, and administrative questions. Would use of categories result in more lengthy legal proceedings? What degree of certainty of scientific information is needed on which to base a category? Will the use of categories result in lower costs to industry for testing chemicals? Could the use of categories improve communication about chemical hazards to users of chemicals? These and other questions will need to be examined before EPA can use categories in a systematic way.

The shortage of testing facilities and qualified professionals argues for an international effort to avoid unproductive duplication in testing. An international testing priorities list might be developed, perhaps by an agency similar to the International Agency for Research on Cancer. Work might then be divided among nations by agreement either that different nations each take major responsibility for testing certain chemicals, or that different types of testing for a given chemical be divided among nations. A system based on existing institutes, which are coordinated from an international center with access to technical experts, may be a feasible approach. However, for this venture to succeed, a number of conditions must be fulfilled. The participating institutes must have guarantees that they will obtain the necessary budget over a long period of time, and they must incorporate experts from all relevant disciplines. In addition, a means must be found to provide access to data while protecting proprietary rights of manufacturers. Further, flexibility in both programs and decision-making processes will be needed to accommodate, on short notice, additional work and the changing needs of countries.

Chapter III

Assessing Hazard

Some chemicals are necessary to life. Many are capable of altering life processes. The study of the interactions between chemicals and life forms, including humans, is a complex scientific area (pharmacology, toxicology, and ecotoxicology) that recognizes many pathways and mechanisms by which effects may occur. Toxicology,[1] including ecotoxicology, is concerned with hazard assessment: determination of the nature and likelihood of adverse effects of chemicals to humans, other organisms, and ecosystems.

Contributions from the discipline of toxicology are indispensable to social judgments that balance the benefits society derives from the use of toxic chemicals against the hazards these chemicals present under conditions of proper use or misuse, and disposal. The professional toxicologist is generally not responsible for social judgments, but is concerned with hazard and the probability of its occurrence.

The importance of environmental factors in inducing some chronic noncommunicable diseases, particularly cancer, is now widely recognized. These diseases may be attributable to diet, alcohol, tobacco, and agents innate to the environment such as sunlight. But increasing numbers of examples establish a link between some chemical contaminants and adverse effects on human health and the environment.[2] Indeed, the health of future populations is also at issue, since years or even decades may elapse between exposure to seemingly innocuous agents and the onset of adverse effects induced by such exposure.

Toxicology is both a scientific discipline and, like medicine, an art that is practiced. Classic toxicological testing calls for exposure to graded doses of a chemical under carefully controlled conditions, and examination of the effects caused by the chemical immediately and over time. It can involve development and use of standardized laboratory test procedures. The intent of such tests may be a study of the validity of a scientific hypothesis, the development of still further refined tests, or the provision of data for assessment of the hazard posed by the chemical to human health and the environment. In this last task, hazard assessment, toxicology is an empirical rather than a theoretical science—since laboratory tests are often only remote surrogates for the real circumstances under which hazard may occur.

In the case of tests to establish physical and chemical properties of chemicals, the results are usually quantifiable and reproducible within closely defined limits. For toxicity testing this is not so. While some expressions of toxicity can be quantified, the numerical results are fully valid only for the condition of study in which they were obtained. The term "adverse effect" is itself imprecise. Living organisms show a range of physiological activity that can be regarded as normal. An "adverse effect" is by definition outside the normal range. The normal range is defined on the basis of measured values found in a group of organisms. An individual with a value outside this range may be showing an abnormal effect or may be a normal individual with a test response outside the normal range. Alternatively, a sensitive individual with a response within the normal range may still be experiencing adverse effects.

An interest in the potentially toxic effects to humans and the environment of a particular commercial chemical can only be satisfied definitively by knowing the actual effects of that chemical on man and the environment under the actual circumstances encountered in use of the chemical. Particularly when considering the introduction of new commercial chemicals, however, there is generally no prior human or environmental experience on which to judge the kinds of adverse effects the chemicals may cause. Some other approach is needed. In practice, hazard assessments are usually based on data obtained under carefully controlled laboratory conditions by dosing organisms with a chemical, by studying the effects of the chemical on cell cultures, and by physicochemical tests. These tests permit inferences to be drawn that depend on extrapolation, from the surrogate test systems and models, to circumstances of actual exposure to chemicals by human populations and the natural environment.

In recent years a growing body of research and expert scientific opinion has held that animal tests can provide a scientifically sound basis for assessing potential risk of a chemical substance to humans. This view has been accepted by many official organizations,[3] including the World Health Organisation, the U.S. National Academy of Sciences and National Cancer Institute, and the German National Research Council. Often, animal test data are the sole basis for determining toxicity of chemical substances, since epidemiologic data are difficult to gather and often are insensitive indicators of effects. Moreover, there is an obvious ethical barrier to consciously using human volunteers for the testing of a new chemical compound. There is also interest for ethical reasons in minimizing the use of animals in laboratory tests by using alternative procedures wherever possible—for example, mathematical models, chemical assays, and tests with lower organisms.

Ecotoxicological tests performed in the laboratory also serve as surrogates for what will happen under natural conditions. Extrapolations from these tests, however, must take into account that actual effects are influenced by a wide variety of factors such as seasonal differences and the host of complex interactions in real environments that can affect the distribution of a chemical in air, water, and soil.

Some kinds of laboratory tests are "better" than others in the sense that they correlate better with actual experience. Tests are generally designed to reveal adverse effects of particular kinds or under particular circumstances. For example, acute toxicity tests are designed to yield information about lethal effects due to a single large dose of a chemical. Other tests, so-called chronic toxicity tests, are used to assess the long-term prospects for injury due to repeated administration of smaller doses over a long period of time. (Some tests, called subchronic tests or sub-acute tests, are of intermediate duration—generally up to about three months in rodents, or equivalent to approximately 10 percent of the test species' normal lifespan.) In general, subchronic and chronic tests tend to be more expensive than acute tests, and obviously take longer. Accordingly, there is a need for shorter tests that are good surrogates for the long-term tests.

There is, once again, a question of setting priorities. Many different kinds of tests need to be performed and their results studied if hazards are to be assessed, since no one test can predict the wide range of potential adverse effects. Economics, time, and limited availability of trained toxicologists make it literally impossible to test all commercial chemicals—even all new chemicals about to be commercialized—for all potential toxic effects. A program for hazard assessment requires selection of certain effects for more attention than others, and in some instances the use of short-term surrogates for some of the longer and more resource-intensive studies.

Hazard assessment, then, usually requires laboratory testing, and the selection of those tests that are most appropriate for the chemical under the circumstances of its intended commercialization. This chapter provides an outline of testing practices, criteria for use of particular tests in assessment of hazard, and the international ramifications of these matters.

TOXICITY AND EXPOSURE

A chemical's toxicity to a living organism may be defined as its capacity to cause injury. Toxicity is not a single parameter like molecular weight, but represents the totality of adverse effects that can be produced when an organism is exposed to a chemical by different routes, at various doses, and over a range of time durations. Thus, a description of toxicity includes the organism, the dose, the route, the time over which administration took place, the type and severity of effects and their development over time. A strenuous effort is made in laboratory tests to exclude all influences on the outcome other than those caused by the chemical under the standardized conditions of the investigation.

A chemical that moves into the environment can affect people on its first passage—through occupational exposure or by release from products, for example. In some instances, exposures associated with uses of products are intentional and accepted, as with drugs and food additives. In other cases, exposure is not essential to the proper functioning of products, though not unexpected in normal product use (this is the case with solvents in paints and paint removers, and chemicals in clothing). In still other instances, exposure is the result of product misuse.

People may not know that they are being exposed to chemicals—for example, by extracting lead from ceramic glazes on dishes, or inhaling asbestos from deteriorating building materials. Normal living spaces offer complex and multiple opportunities for exposure.

Further, chemicals may also be released into the broader physical environment—through air, water or soil—where many kinds of animals and plants are exposed. Distribution of a chemical to the physical environment may occur deliberately (as in the case of pesticides). It may be incidental to product use (as in the case of aerosol propellants and paint solvents). It may be incidental to the manufacture, processing, or disposal of a chemical or a product of which it is a part. Or it may occur through purely natural processes such as volcanic eruptions and erosion of rocks.

Moreover, chemicals may be reconcentrated, particularly through the food chain, so that people are again exposed. Or new substances may be produced by chemical and biochemical processes in the environment. For example, inorganic mercury can be transformed biochemically by micro-organisms in the environment to the more toxic organic compound methylmercury.[4]

The major routes for human exposure to chemicals are inhalation, ingestion, and skin contact. These routes and their relative significance are affected by the properties of the chemical.

Inhalation is an important direct route of human exposure because of the large volume of air that passes through the lungs and the ready absorption there of many chemicals. Inhaled particles penetrate the respiratory tract to an extent that varies with their size. Particles in the bronchial system can also be transported back to the pharynx and then swallowed, so inhalation exposure may be linked to ingestion.

Ingestion of toxic quantities of chemicals can be accidental or intentional. The most common situation is long-term repeated exposure to contaminants, residues, or additives in food and water at dosages too low to cause acute effects.

The *dermal* route—through the surface of the skin—can be of considerable significance in the occupational field, but may also be important to the general population because of contact with personal-care products such as cosmetics and chemicals that may be released from such products as clothing, upholstery, shoes, and printed paper.

TYPES OF TESTS

There are three major areas of testing—for physicochemical properties, for degradation and accumulation in the environment, and for toxicological, including ecotoxicological, effects. The state of the art is summarized here. More extensive descriptions can be found in the reports of the OECD Chemicals Testing Programme.[5]

Physicochemical Information

The kind of toxicological testing that is appropriate for a chemical will depend on such factors as:

- chemical identity, including chemical structure and impurities;

- physical state (gas, liquid, solid), including melting point, boiling point, and vapor pressure;

- solubility and partition, including water solubility, fat solubility, and partition between water and a nonmiscible solvent (usually n-octanol);

- general physical properties, including density, surface tension, and acidity (pH);

- stability—thermal, in air, to light, in acidic and basic media, to microorganisms, and explosivity.

This information is valuable in many ways. First, chemical structure (even in the absence of other information) may suggest the nature of the hazard associated with a substance by so-called "structure-activity relationships." For example, if a chemical is a high-molecular-weight polymer, it is not likely to be absorbed through the skin. Or, if toxicological effects have been associated with a structural feature common to certain chemicals, related chemicals with that feature might be expected to produce similar effects. Thus, many small chlorinated hydrocarbons have been associated with liver damage, while nitrosamines have been associated with cancer. Structure-activity relations will undoubtedly be the subject of continued interest and study, since they are useful in making a first estimate of effects that are likely to occur and in planning toxicological test programs. They also offer the potential for judging hazard without the need for toxicological testing of every member of a given family of chemicals.

Second, such factors as physical state are useful in planning a toxicological test program. Obviously, a material that is not a gas at normal temperatures and pressures is unlikely to be a candidate for an inhalation toxicology program, unless the material is a finely divided mist or (respirable) dust. Other examples are even more obvious: a substance such as metallic sodium that reacts violently on contact with water is not a good candidate for an oral feeding study; neither is a strong acid that burns on contact.

Third, physicochemical properties can determine environmental distribution. A water-soluble, nonvolatile chemical is more likely to be present in the environment in waterways, lakes, and oceans than is a water-insoluble, volatile compound. The latter would likely be present as a pollutant in air. Octanol/water partition coefficients (measuring the distribution of a chemical, at equilibrium, between n-octanol and water phases) correlate with the tendency of chemicals to be found in fatty tissue, and to increase in concentration as one progresses up the food chain—a phenomenon known as bioconcentration. Test data on stability can suggest whether a chemical is likely to be persistent in the environment.

Fourth, physicochemical properties can directly indicate hazard from, for example, explosivity or acidity.

For these reasons, it is desirable to obtain a knowledge of chemical structure and some physical chemical properties before embarking on a toxicological testing program.

Degradation and Accumulation

To determine the risk from a chemical that is released to the environment, it is necessary to estimate the chemical's concentration and distribution in the environment. Use and disposal information and the substance's physicochemical properties give some clues, but, to make more realistic estimates, it is helpful to know how the chemical degrades in air, water, and soil as well as how it accumulates in organisms and in soil. In a December 1979 report,[6] an OECD Expert Group on Degradation/Accumulation focused on the following four areas of concern for testing.

Biodegradation in Water. Problems with detergents that had not been removed in sewage treatment and caused foaming led to the development of tests for biodegradability in the 1960s. The OECD group on biodegradation and accumulation recommends specific tests at three levels to determine a substance's biodegradation in water—ready biodegradability, indicating whether a substance biodegrades rapidly; inherent biodegradability, indicating whether a chemical has the potential to degrade under favorable conditions such as prolonged exposure to microorganisms; and simulation tests to provide evidence of rates of degradation in specific environments, as during biological treatment or in a lake.

Photodegradation. The most significant degradation process for organic chemicals that enter the atmosphere is photodegradation, either directly (by absorption of energy from sunlight) or indirectly (by the action of sunlight to produce reactive chemicals from the natural constituents of the atmosphere, which in turn react with organic chemicals). Screening tests can indicate whether photodegradation is likely. In general, chemicals that readily biodegrade or decompose in water will not accumulate to a sufficient degree in the atmosphere to require testing for photodegradation.

Bioaccumulation in Organisms. Chemicals can accumulate directly or indirectly in organisms. For aquatic species such as fish, direct accumulation of chemicals from water predominates over indirect accumulation through the foodchain. For terrestrial species, indirect bioaccumulation through the food chain is the more important route. Physicochemical tests (water solubility, volatility, and n-octanol/water partition coefficient) as well as biodegradability tests indicate whether special bioaccumulation tests are needed. Fish are the recommended animal species for bioaccumulation testing.

Degradation and Accumulation in Soils. The fate of chemicals in soils and sediments is of importance since contamination of soils can be long lasting and difficult to reverse. Tests are recommended for chemicals that are not readily biodegraded in an aquatic environment and that can be expected to contaminate soils as a result of their anticipated use or disposal. A variety of tests are considered, starting with biodegradability in soil (under aerobic conditions to simulate shallow soil layers where oxygen is readily available, though anaerobic conditions should be considered if leaching to deeper soils is likely). In addition, studies of accumulation and mobility in soils as well as of abiotic degradation in sterilized soils may be considered.

Toxicological Effects

Acute toxicity. Acute toxicity is investigated to identify the degree of immediate hazard posed by a chemical and to provide information on specific toxic effects, the mode of action, and toxicity relative to other chemicals. This investigation also provides useful information in planning longer-term tests. An acute toxicity test gives information on potential lethality. It will, at one extreme, identify those chemicals that are highly dangerous, for which adverse effects occur with small doses within a short time after exposure, or, at the other extreme, those where the lethal dose is so large that, in practical terms, there is no likelihood of immediate adverse effects.

The commonly used routes for administering toxicity tests are oral, inhalational, and dermal. For solids and liquids, the oral route is generally investigated first, to provide basic information. This may be supplemented by tests that use one or both of the other routes. For gases, the inhalation route is used, while in the case of volatile substances that route is normally the second to be investigated, after oral studies. The dermal route is significant for many chemicals, but it is also difficult to investigate in a meaningful manner.

One result of a suitably designed oral test for acute toxicity is establishment of a median lethal dose or LD50 value, derived by applying statistical methods to a test that uses groups of animals exposed to a range of doses. (Median lethal concentrations, LC50 values, are obtained from inhalation toxicity tests.) The LD50 value is the theoretical dose that will kill 50 percent of an exposed group. It is a much abused and misused figure and must not be regarded as an absolute number that identifies with precision the toxicity of a chemical. LD50 (and LC50) values for a chemical can vary widely because acute toxicity is influenced by a large number of test conditions, such as the species and strain of test animals, the breeding and nutrition of the test animals, and their age.

Since LD50 and LC50 values have practical applications in the classification of chemicals in terms of relative toxicity (which can involve intercomparison of test results obtained at different times in different laboratories), there is an ongoing interest in standardizing acute toxicity tests. There is comparable interest in standardizing the other test procedures described below. Although there can be variation in the determination of the physico-chemical properties of a substance, depending on the conditions of the test, the variation in animal test results is inherently greater—the health and mortality of living creatures being subject to factors such as the vagaries of heredity, individual history, and the stressfulness of the circumstances under which tests are performed. Because of the complexity of the circumstances that must be dealt with in toxicological testing, it is usually considered wasteful, even impractical scientifically, to standardize every detail of testing; a reasoned flexibility of approach is necessary. Nonetheless, a substantial degree of uniformity of approach is possible and desirable in most instances.

To illustrate what can be done in this regard, an OECD expert group, in reaching agreement on guidelines for acute oral toxicity testing, concluded that test conditions should conform to certain guidelines.[7] For example:

- Although several mammalian species may be used, the rat is recommended. Commonly used laboratory strains should be employed.
- The weight variation in animals should not exceed ±20 percent.
- At least ten rodents should be used at each dose (5 female and 5 male).
- At least three dose levels should be chosen, spaced appropriately to produce test groups with a range of toxic effects and mortality rates.
- The temperature of the experimental animal room should be 22°C (±3°) and the relative humidity 30-70 percent.
- Where the lighting is artificial, the sequence should be 12 hours light, 12 hours dark.
- Animals should be fasted prior to administration of the chemical. For the rat, food should be withheld overnight.
- For feeding, conventional laboratory diets may be used with an unlimited supply of drinking water.
- The observation period should be at least 14 days.
- Observations should be made frequently during the first day and twice daily, at least four hours apart (once each morning and afternoon), as far as practicable thereafter.

The OECD guidelines also cover many other procedural aspects of the test (including observations at cageside, and studies of pathological changes) that can influence its cost and results. These items illustrate what needs to be specified in a generally acceptable test protocol, but there is still much room for variations of such details as the particulars of diet and postmortem examination.

Local effects on skin and eye. The physical form (for example, liquid, dust), the properties of a chemical, and its use pattern can suggest that local skin and eye effects should be studied. Substances determined to be strongly acidic or alkaline need not be studied for skin and eye effects undiluted, because they can reliably be predicted to produce marked effects. In these cases, any tests would be directed toward determining the dilution that does not produce effects. When indicated, these investigations should be performed early, since accidental skin and eye contamination may occur during manufacture and in the subsequent handling and use of a chemical. The results of skin studies should be assessed before eye studies are started (a chemical that is an irritant or corrosive to the skin will usually have even more marked effects on the eye).

Allergic sensitization. Some chemicals that cause little, if any, response on first exposure create a sensitized state in the individual exposed, so that later exposures cause an allergic response, for example, a dermatitis. The rash caused in some people by exposure to poison ivy is an allergic sensitization response.

Sensitization responses, particularly of the skin and respiratory tract, affect a significant proportion of the human population and are of considerable importance in assessing occupational and general consumer risks. It has been estimated that 10 percent of the human population has a defective immunological response that produces an enhanced susceptibility to allergenic chemicals.[8]

A word of caution: though laboratory animal tests are frequently conducted solely for the purpose of estimating likely effects on human health, the validity of such extrapolation is sometimes in doubt. Constraints imposed by the current state of the art of toxicology often lead to hazard assessment on the basis of tests that may only imperfectly mimic human responses. Nonetheless, toxicological tests will often yield clues that lead to more extensive toxicological evaluation and can justify caution in proceeding with commercial use of products.

Interpretation of skin sensitization tests and extrapolation of the results to humans must be made in this context, with a high degree of caution. The wide range of individual susceptibility and response and the range of results obtained with different animal test systems add considerable uncertainty to assessment of this form of toxicity.

Guinea pigs are conventionally used in such tests. The OECD guidelines for skin sensitization point out that substances that are strong sensitizers in guinea pigs also cause a substantial number of sensitization reactions in man, whereas weak sensitizers in guinea pigs may or may not cause reactions in man.

Subchronic toxicity. One form of human exposure to chemicals is in repeated small doses that may not produce any immediate toxic effects. However, depending on how the body reacts, this exposure may lead to increasing levels of the chemical in the body, to storage in specific tissues, and ultimately to the development of toxic effects.

In a subchronic toxicity study, experimental animals are exposed over a period of time to repeated daily doses well below those that are immediately fatal—for example, 1 percent or less of LD50. The results of these studies can provide information on toxicity, identify target organs, and determine the reversibility or irreversibility of toxic effects. As will be discussed later in this chapter, it can be argued that most substances to which humans will be exposed should be considered for initial testing in a base set of tests—a so-called minimum premarket set of data (see p. 44)—that includes subchronic testing.

In addition, information on doses and effects derived from this type of study is extremely important in establishing suitable doses for longer-duration studies. In a sense, subchronic testing is a gateway into exploration of the effects of chronic exposure to chemicals. Many different kinds of effects may come into focus as a result of subchronic testing, and there are many different pathways along which further test programs can proceed. Scientific judgment and case-by-case consideration of study plans become increasingly important as one leaves the province of the base set and proceeds into follow-up tests, where there are increasingly large numbers of options for designing study plans specially tailored to best reveal the toxic effects of a substance.

Chronic toxicity. Acute and subchronic toxicity tests are of limited value in predicting possible adverse effects from prolonged administration, because chemicals can produce additional or different toxic responses when administered over a long period. Also, the development of animals as they age can modify the nature and degree of toxic response. Chronic toxicity tests, extending up to the life-span of an animal, can identify toxic effects that are missed by acute and subchronic tests.

The terminology used to describe acute and chronic toxicity tests and effects can be confusing. Acute tests customarily involve exposure to a single dose, though occasionally the dose may be divided into parts that are all given over a short period of time. The effects may be acute and immediate, or chronic (persisting over a long period of time). Many soldiers during World War I suffered subsequent chronic effects from a single acute exposure to mustard gas. In contrast, chronic tests involve administration of repeated doses of a chemical over a long period of time. The effects of the chemical may be seen soon after dosing commences or may appear only much later. Chronic or acute effects may be irreversible, and persist for the lifetime of the animal, or reversible, disappearing in time.

Chronic and subchronic toxicity tests have been used to establish so-called "no-toxic-effect" dosage levels below which no toxic effects are expected. These levels have been used to establish so-called "threshold limit values" for occupational exposure to chemicals and to determine acceptable daily intakes for residues or additives in food, and other tolerance limits.

For some kinds of chronic effects—cancer, birth defects, and genetic changes in particular—the concept of a no-toxic-effect dosage level is the subject of hot controversy, since mechanisms by which such effects are postulated to occur suggest that even the smallest dosage level may initiate processes that lead to injury or disease in animals or humans.

For other kinds of effects, there is more widespread agreement that there are "no-toxic-effect" levels for chemicals—at least in well-controlled laboratory tests, using animals that are homogeneous in their heredity, life histories, and health. It is in the extrapolation to humans that such no-effect levels are increasingly brought into question, since the human condition is extremely diverse. People are heterogeneous in heredity, life history, and present health. Some people are inherently more sensitive to injury than others; hence, threshold limits that can be expected to protect most people may be inadequate for others. It is, in part, for this reason that threshold limit values and acceptable daily intake figures normally are chosen after applying a "safety factor" to no-toxic-effect levels from animal studies. Even such conservative approaches may still not provide adequate protection for the most sensitive people or the most sensitive population groups.[9]

Carcinogenicity. Cancer is a disease that is serious in its incidence, its progressive nature, and the difficulties of treatment. It involves heritable alterations in cells, that is, alterations that can be transmitted as the cells divide and proliferate. Further, there may be a long latency period between exposure to a chemical and tumor formation caused by the exposure. Though there may or may not be reversibility or correctibility of effects at early stages, all that can now be said with confidence is that "the lower the exposure, the less the risk."

To identify the carcinogenic potential of a chemical, a study over the life-span of test animals is still considered the best approach. High doses of a substance are usually required in such tests so that statistically significant responses can be achieved without the need for inordinately large groups of animals. Mutagenicity tests, discussed below, are increasingly of interest as initial screens of carcinogenic potential.

Life-span studies for determination of either carcinogenic potential or chronic general toxicity call for the maintenance and examination of animals over an extended period of time. Each kind of test is conventionally based on extensive preplanning in which animal selection, animal care, dosing, and examination for effects are specified in detail. Carcinogenicity and chronic toxicity tests may be conducted separately or as a single, combined study.

Regulatory actions taken by U.S. federal agencies in the past few years have reopened the question of the validity of using animal species for assessing carcinogenic risk to human populations. A recent draft report[10] prepared by the Toxic Substances Strategy Committee, convened by the

White House Council on Environmental Quality, reaffirms the fundamental soundness of using animal tests for determining a chemical's carcinogenic potential to humans.

Mutagenicity. A chemical mutagen produces a change in a cell that can be inherited (a heritable change). If this change affects a germ cell (sperm or ovum), the change can be transmitted to succeeding generations. Human defects of genetic origin can range from gross malformations to impairment of a single enzyme system.

Mutagenicity testing is one of the areas in toxicology that is experiencing rapid scientific development and technical innovation. Many tests for "mutagenicity screening" have been developed using microorganisms, mammalian cells in culture, or whole animals. These tests examine the various ways in which a chemical can interact with the genetic apparatus of a cell and produce a heritable change. The best known is the so-called Ames test,[11] named after Bruce Ames who developed it, which uses a bacterial test system (*Salmonella typhimurium*) with the addition of a mammalian liver preparation to provide metabolic actions like those occurring in an animal; there are also numerous other tests in varying stages of development.

It is generally accepted that no single rapid screening test provides definitive information on the mutagenicity of a chemical; hence, the emphasis is on a battery of different kinds of mutagenicity tests. It should also be noted that in many cases genetic damage is induced not by the chemical itself but by the products formed as the chemical is metabolized.

The keen interest in mutagenicity screening tests is, in part, due to good correlations that have been observed between the results of some of these tests and life-span animal carcinogenicity tests.[12] Mutagenicity screening tests are very much less expensive—as little as 1 percent or so[13]—and very much faster than life-span animal tests. Naturally, mutagenicity screening tests are for these reasons attractive. A number of testing laboratories, and pharmaceutical and chemical companies are starting to incorporate these screening tests routinely in their testing programs.

The OECD expert committee report on this subject recommends that in most instances a few such tests be included as part of the pre-market data set, using tests based on each of two principal modes of action (gene damage and chromosomal alteration). The report states:

> Positive responses in mutagenicity tests present a warning signal and indicate that further work should be considered involving other mutagenic test systems to evaluate further mutagenic potential. As mutations may be one mechanism for cancer induction, positive mutagenic responses may also indicate that potential for carcinogenesis should be investigated.[14]

Positive results in these screening tests should be seen as "red flags." This means that either the investigator accepts the results at face value (assuming the results can be reproduced) and considers the substance mutagenic/carcinogenic on a qualitative basis, or that these preliminary results should lead to more extensive testing to arrive at a more definitive estimate of the risk posed by the substance.

Fertility and reproduction. Investigations in this area are increasingly important because it is now known that many chemicals can affect fertility and reproduction, often in an insidious manner. Effects on fertility can range from a marginally decreased reproduction rate to complete sterility. Fertility can be affected in both males and females.

Teratogenicity. Teratogenicity involves adverse effects to the embryo and fetus during development because of exposure to a chemical. The effects can range from gross malformations to barely detectable behavioral deficiencies. The large numbers of women in the child-bearing period of life who are employed in jobs where exposure to chemicals occurs highlights the need for knowledge in this area.

Absorption, metabolism, and toxicokinetics. Because many of the adverse effects of a chemical are related to the quantity actually absorbed by a living organism (as opposed to the dose administered), or to byproducts produced by metabolic modification of the original chemical, investigations of these possibilities are frequently of importance in exploring the mechanisms of toxicity.

Metabolism is a necessary natural function that can modify chemicals so they can be used by the body or rendered innocuous or less biologically active before excretion. Metabolic processes can also work the other way and produce products more toxic than their predecessor. Metabolism is a complex process with wide species variation, and alternative pathways which differ in their capacities to metabolize chemicals. A detailed knowledge of events in this area is highly desirable in evaluating toxicity and extrapolating from other animal species to humans, but it is frequently a complex, costly, and time-consuming exercise. Because it involves the specific characteristics of given substances, there are few standard guidelines for this kind of study.

Ecotoxicological Effects

Ecotoxicity deals with the adverse effects of chemicals on biological systems in the environment. Although, because of the large number of biological systems and their many interactions, ecotoxicity testing is inherently more complex than toxicity testing for assessing hazards to human health, it can be broken down into investigations of adverse effects on representative micro-organisms, plants, and animals—in aquatic and ter-restial environments.

In studies of effects in the terrestrial environment representative mam-malian, bird, and plant species may be used, while fish and plant species can be used to study aquatic environments. In some cases, it is also practical to create representative soil systems in the laboratory and to examine the effects of chemicals on these. It is necessary to consider carefully whether the species selected are representative of, or good surrogates for, those that may be affected in actual environments.

The response of an ecosystem to a chemical depends on complex interactions involving many species. Often, tests using only a single species may not reveal the nature or magnitude of the hazard. For this reason, microcosms are sometimes devised which involve construction in the laboratory of a sample terrestial or aquatic ecosystem. Efforts are being made to develop standard model ecosystem tests.

Ecotoxicological testing may be performed in the laboratory or in the field. The two approaches can be used to complement each other. When toxic effects are found in the laboratory, they can signal the need to check for effects under more natural conditions.

Environmental monitoring, showing widespread environmental dis-tribution of a chemical, may indicate the need for laboratory tests. Simula-tions (using models of parts of ecosystems in the laboratory, using con-trolled field situations such as a test pond, or using mathematical models) are yielding information on how ecosystems function. However, they are not now well enough developed to use for routine testing of chemical effects.

Ecotoxicological tests differ from animal tests performed to assess toxic effects on humans:

- The effect on the individual is of ultimate concern in human toxicol-ogy, while in ecotoxicology the major focus is on the effects on populations and communities and the overall functioning of ecosystems.

- In animal tests to assess effects on humans, the dose is usually administered directly to individual test animals. In ecotoxicology, the chemical is put into the water, air, or soil where it may be degraded, transformed, or adsorbed over a period of time; dose in this case may depend on the nature and importance of these factors.

As in animal tests to assess human effects, there are ecotoxicological tests for acute and chronic effects. An acute test is short in relation to the life-span of the test species. A sub-chronic test lasts at least 10 percent of a generation for a species with a life cycle of at least a year, such as a fish, and a chronic test lasts at least one generation.

The OECD Ecotoxicology Expert Group received 122 testing methodologies in response to its request for standardized descriptions of existing accepted tests. These tests have not been validated, a step the OECD Group recommends be taken. Some of the tests are well enough developed to be used routinely. This is particularly true for tests on aquatic species. There are also tests using terrestrial invertebrates such as the earthworm as well as some for higher plants.

The OECD Expert group suggests three tests for a first level of ecotoxicological testing. A 96-hour fish LC50 test would measure the toxicity of a chemical added to water by testing how many fish die or show other effects in a specific time period. A 14-day LC50 test on daphnia would test the effect of the chemical on mortality, growth, and reproduction. A test on algae would assess the chemical's potential to limit plant growth. The goal of these tests is to get an indication of the range of effects. The OECD Expert Group report suggests that it is more important to do the tests on a variety of species at this stage, to get an idea of the variability of effects, rather than to test extensively a specific species. Two other levels of testing are suggested if the results of the first group of tests, or production, use, and disposal patterns, or other information, such as low degradability, raise enough doubts to suggest that further testing is desirable.

The OECD Expert Group found that several kinds of tests were not well represented in the test methodologies submitted. They included simulated or actual field testing, testing of terrestrial species, microbiological testing, testing for synergistic effects, and testing for effects on relationships among species. The need for testing in systems with many species is illustrated by the problems chemicals have created by interfering with predator-prey balances. For example, if certain mammals or birds are killed by a chemical, rodents may increase.

Ecotoxicology also has a major difficulty in determining whether observed effects are ecologically significant. These effects may include changes in the developmental stages of a species from germination and birth through reproduction and death. There are also secondary effects to be considered such as changes in behavior or pigmentation. An ecosystem may be stimulated, as in eutrophication, or retarded. Generally, persistent and irreversible effects in the functioning of an ecosystem are of most concern, but, given the ability of ecosystems to adapt and repair themselves, it is not always easy to categorize something as irreversible or significant.[15]

Other Toxicological Effects

The preceding description of toxicological and ecotoxicological testing is necessarily incomplete; there are many other kinds of testing procedures. Further, toxicological practice is not static. Testing programs today are more likely to emphasize cancer, gene mutations, and birth defects than did the programs planned during the 1950s. However, it is already clear that still other facets of toxicology—for example, behavioral toxicology, immunotoxicology, and further development of ecotoxicology—will receive more emphasis in the years ahead. New tests are being devised and new effects will need to be added to those now studied as a matter of course.

It would appear wise neither to lock toxicological practice into a framework that precludes usage of newer tests and procedures nor to so emphasize the need for flexibility as to frustrate legitimate needs for regularity, standardization, and predictability of testing.

TEST PROGRAMS FOR CHEMICALS

There are many tests that can be used to assess the toxic potential of a chemical, and thus there is a large range of possible testing programs, and of views about what program should be adopted. An argument at one extreme may hold that only chemicals intended to affect life processes (for example, drugs and pesticides) should be tested for toxicity. At the other extreme, some have argued that to obtain a sufficiently detailed toxicological characterization of any chemical for an adequate assessment of hazard, most of the test areas and tests outlined above, with probable additions, are required.

Neither alternative is wholly satisfactory. In the first case, many or most chemicals can be toxic under certain conditions, underscoring the saying that "it is the dose that makes the poison." The second alternative, that of the full panoply of tests, has some attractions, but against these must be weighed time and cost factors. A practical approach lies somewhere between these two extremes: a testing program should be capable of identifying a serious or important toxic hazard to human health or the environment at an early stage in the development of a chemical, before significant human exposure and before the chemical is released in significant amounts into the environment.

Because chemicals differ in their toxicity, it can be argued that each should be treated as an individual case, with a testing program devised specifically to fit its particular characteristics. By this approach, which is favored by many scientists, each test should be conducted as a scientific study and seen as part of a unique investigation of toxic effects for the chemical in question. This requires skilled toxicological assessment at every stage. The approach is the most satisfying in toxicological and scientific terms, but it is most demanding in time and toxicological expertise, both of which are in short supply.

Standardized Programs

A regularized testing system, with a rigidly defined group of tests for all chemicals and standard test methods, stands at the other extreme from treating each chemical as an individual case. A standardized program has attractions for the regulator, and for those who are concerned that flexible requirements might legitimize shoddy work or be used in a discriminatory way against imports (that is, to protect domestic manufacturers unfairly by arbitrarily requiring more complete testing of imported chemicals). Also, well-defined testing requirements can appeal to the developer of new chemicals, because it is much easier to comply with testing requirements if they are explicitly stated beforehand. In toxicological terms, this approach can lead to expenditure of effort on development of useless information; it also runs the risk of seeing certain tests not performed in some instances where they may be desirable. If carried to an extreme that forces use of inappropriate or obsolete testing procedures, a rigidly defined system for testing can lead to the generation of misleading information.

An intermediate approach is clearly called for, in which guidelines are used in a manner that provides the flexibility to add or omit tests and to use unconventional protocols, whenever there is good reason to do so. Further, since there needs to be consideration of each of the several kinds of effects that are studied using different kinds of tests, a group of tests (a base set) will be essential in most instances.

Base Set and Tiered Testing

Where toxicity testing is directed toward acquiring information about hazard to human health, there is a move toward defining a minimum amount of information, referred to variously as the "base set," "tier 0," "level 0," or "minimum pre-market set of data (MPD)." Most or all of the following are usually included: acute toxicity, local effects on skin and eye, potential for allergic sensitization, short-term tests for mutagenicity (which may also be predictive of carcinogenicity), a short-term repeated dose (subchronic) study, selected physical and chemical information, degradation/accumulation data, and ecotoxicological tests with fish, daphnia, and algae. A pre-market set of data developed within the OECD[16] includes all of these elements as well as chemical identification data, production/use/disposal data, analytical methods, and recommended precautions and emergency measures. Principles of tiered testing are also fundamental to the Directive 79/831/EEC.

If there is no indication of a toxic problem at the base-set stage, the need for further testing to provide reassurance or to examine marginal effects has been linked to the following considerations described in a 1978 report[17], based on discussions by experts from industry, environmental public interest groups, and academic institutions in the United States:

- volume of production;
- anticipated or actual use, and environmental or human exposure;
- nature of the potential hazard;
- physicochemical properties;
- structure-activity relationships.

This kind of tiered or hierarchical test program, which appears to be a cost-effective system for assessing toxicity of chemical substances, starts with relatively simple and inexpensive tests and proceeds to increasingly more complex, lengthy, and costly tests. The basic concept is increasingly being recognized by regulatory bodies as an acceptable procedure for assessing toxicity.

A tiered testing approach requires flexibility at both ends. For the tier at the low end (the base set), one needs flexibility to add additional tests suggested by structure-activity relationships, and to delete tests that are inappropriate or unnecessary for scientific reasons. For example, materials highly reactive with water can be excluded from animal feeding studies.

Furthermore, one needs flexibility to take into account chemicals that are used only in ways that do not present much potential for human or environmental exposure, such as substances used only as reaction intermediates at low volumes in closed systems.

Other exclusions may be acceptable on the basis of cost in relation to expected risks. In these instances, one cannot state with confidence that serious adverse effects of chemicals would not have been found had the testing been done. On the contrary, the exclusions are based on the expectation that the public health risks would be limited even if they were found, and the judgment that such risks to the public are acceptable. The Directive 79/831/EEC, by exempting polymers and materials produced at less than one ton per year from testing requirements, in effect expresses the judgment that exemption of these substances from testing is reasonable. The judgment can be viewed as involving questions of cost-effectiveness, a recognition that producers of small-volume chemicals cannot economically bear much testing burden, and a desire to establish easily understood exemptions. Low-volume chemicals are not necessarily low-risk chemicals, but volume of production is one key factor in determining potential for human and environmental exposure; that factor is in many ways the one most readily measured and understood.

There has been much controversy about a base set or minimum premarket set of data (MPD). Most would agree that certain kinds of toxicological tests, such as acute toxicity and skin irritation tests, sensibly belong in an early grouping of tests at the start of a hazard evaluation. However, for some participants in the debate, the term "base set" has become an emotion-laden phrase evoking images of rigid testing requirements regardless of reason and logic. This objection can be met by careful definition of what a base set is meant to be.

The report of the OECD Expert Group on short- and long-term testing articulates the following important points: "The MPD is generally accepted as a battery of tests to be *considered* [emphasis added] in the initial evaluation of a new chemical." The report goes on to state that "in the case of toxicity tests in the MPD, there is general agreement on the tests involved and the indications for carrying out the tests, but there are also valid exceptions to conducting all of the tests for all of the chemicals . . . In addition, there will be circumstances in which more or different tests are needed for an initial evaluation."[18]

Some exceptions to the base set (MPD)—additions or deletions—can be defined. But the list should expand, as experience is gained in testing an ever-larger number of chemicals intended for use under increasingly diverse circumstances. In effect, a current list of examples of exceptions, already provided by OECD, creates the basis for broadening consensus on the kinds of exceptions that are appropriate, taking science, economics, and attitudes toward risk into account. In so doing, it turns the argument in a most constructive manner toward consideration of necessary exceptions, and away from whether there should be an MPD, thus allowing for agreement on the base-set tests to be considered.

The Directive 79/831/EEC requires base-set testing (subject to exceptions described in Chapter IV) for new chemicals, but also provides exclusions "if it is not technically possible or if it does not appear necessary." It places the burden on the notifier for stating why. A French regulation of May 28, 1979, requires an applicant who does not complete some sections of the notification dossier, or thinks they are irrelevant to his particular case, to state the reasons and to supply the missing information as soon as these reasons cease to apply.

A draft of a German bill is also more specific than the EC Directive. It uses the phrase "is not required in view of the state of scientific knowledge" in place of "does not appear necessary." The German draft also places the burden on the notifier for nonpresentation of information.[19]

Higher Tiers

Professional judgments are unavoidable once the realm of interpreting base-set results is entered. At this point, one must weigh many considerations that have very heavy consequences. There is no cookbook approach possible to the imposition of higher-tiered tests, though a list of additional tests requiring consideration can be used for guidance. Increasing flexibility is needed. Obviously, there needs to be some compromise between scientific perfectionism, cost, the availability of testing resources, and the kinds of testing that are perceived as necessary by the scientist, by the public, and by government officials.

The Directive 79/831/EEC provides wide latitude for judgment about higher-tiered testing, but it does set some firm quantitative limits. Additional testing beyond the base set may be required by a government if the quantity of a substance placed on the market by a notifier reaches a level of 10 tons per year or a total of 50 tons. At 100 tons per year, or 500 tons cumulative, the government must require an additional group of tests "unless in any particular case an alternative scientific study would be preferable." At 1,000 tons per year, or 5,000 tons cumulative, the government will "draw up a programme of tests to be carried out by the notifier in order to enable the competent authority to evaluate the risks of the substance for man and the environment."

Many would argue that exposure is better than production volume as a trigger for additional testing. But exposure is a complex concept, difficult to measure or express in simple terms (See "Exposure and Dosage Assessment" in Chapter V) and, for these reasons, not very useful—at least at this time—as a means of determining when more testing is needed. Although production volume is in many instances a poor surrogate for exposure, it is a specific, simple measure that can be used as a matter of public policy to initiate a tiered system of testing, as illustrated in practical terms by its use in 79/831/EEC.

Government testing of chemicals could be very helpful in terms of filling in gaps—could, in fact, provide an additional means of obtaining test results that might not be available under a straight application of tier-testing rules. This might be construed, however, as transferring responsibility for testing to government, whereas it is generally agreed that responsibility should fall on the manufacturer or importer. One may consider government testing, therefore, as a means, in particular cases, of obtaining information not supplied by manufacturers or importers, and of confirming from time to time the information that is submitted.

What to Test

Either the pure chemical or a technical grade of the chemical—that is, the chemical as actually manufactured and used—can be tested. Testing of the pure grade will aid in intercomparison of results for different chemicals. Testing of technical grades will take into account the influences of impurities, and is highly relevant to risk assessment since most human exposure will be to technical-grade materials and their formulations.

International Harmonization

The Organisation for Economic Cooperation and Development (OECD) is taking the lead in a strong and successful effort to harmonize testing guidelines, principles of good laboratory practices, a minimum pre-marketing set of data, and mutual acceptance of data. In these areas, the OECD has been able to enlist excellent cooperation in establishing working groups comprised of experts from the member nations. The results of this work are setting the stage for internationally harmonious practices. Ongoing and new work of the OECD will set criteria for further testing, monitoring, and assessment (after initial testing and assessment), including "step sequence" testing schemes, methods for hazard assessment, and good laboratory practices—in addition to matters outside the scope of hazard assessment.

International agreement on testing requires consideration of each of four steps:

- First, agreement or cooperation on the acceptance of protocols and good laboratory practices. In other words, how one conducts the tests—what constitutes good test procedures.

- Second, acceptance of the test results themselves, that is, international agreement and cooperation so that the results of tests in one country will be accepted in another country. For example, the results of an Ames mutagenicity test done in Sweden would be accepted in the United States.

- Third, the acceptance of tests for designated effects. One could accept the results of the Ames Test without accepting that it was a good measure for mutagenicity, much less carcinogenicity. So there is a further step or dimension of agreeing that certain kinds of tests are valid measures for certain kinds of effects.

- Fourth, the matter of what effects are of interest, that is the effects that should be evaluated by laboratory tests.

Agreement on these four points would, in effect, constitute international harmonization of testing.

TRANSNATIONAL ACCEPTABILITY OF TEST DATA

One method of improving and advancing the transnational acceptability of test data is through more national and international interlaboratory comparison studies with identical chemicals (ring tests). This approach has been employed in toxicology, notably in the evaluation of the LD50 test, short-term mutagenicity tests, and bioaccumulation tests. The results have confirmed variations between laboratories and have also reduced the area of uncertainty.

In addition to the need for mutual recognition of the qualifications of toxicologists trained in different countries, and of test facilities and accepted test methods, there is also the need for the investigator conducting tests to adhere to good laboratory procedures so as to insure that all test data are reliably obtained and scrupulously reported. In the past, faulty laboratory practices and sloppy record-keeping methods of some contract laboratories and manufacturing companies led to adoption of the Good Laboratory Practice (GLP) Standards by the U.S. Federal Food and Drug Administration (FDA).[20] More recently, the U.S. EPA has also proposed such standards, building on the experience of the FDA. In its proposal, the EPA noted that past abuses by some companies led to:

> [S]elective reporting and underreporting of test results, lack of adherence to specified protocols, inadequate qualification and supervision of personnel, poor animal care procedures, poor record-keeping techniques, and the general failure of sponsors to monitor studies.[21]

The proposed EPA regulation on GLP would include standards for: (a) substance characteristics, including handling and storage of the chemical substances; (b) personnel qualifications, including defining responsibility for the management of the testing facility; (c) the development of an internal laboratory "Quality Assurance Unit," which would provide a mechanism for monitoring ongoing studies; (d) administrative and personnel facilities, including guidance for structural requirements and special handling of volatile and radioactive materials; (e) equipment design, calibration, and maintenance; (f) operation of testing facilities, including proper care and handling of test animals; (g) study design and conduct, including establishment of protocols to assure data quality and integrity; (h) guidance on record keeping, including reporting of study results that reflect complete and accurate representation of actual laboratory experience, and the storage and retrieval of records and data; and (i) inspection of testing facilities, including periodic on-the-premises examination by agency personnel or agents. A comprehensive regulatory program like GLP, when put into practice, should go a long way in providing reliable and accurate data on all test results and should at the same time alleviate any suspicions of wrong-doing on the part of a commercial testing laboratory or a private industrial facility.

An OECD Expert Group[22] has developed Principles of Good Laboratory Practice, for testing in the laboratory and in the field, in four areas: physico-chemical testing; environmental transport, degradation, and accumulation; ecotoxicological studies to evaluate environmental effects; and toxicological studies to evaluate human health effects. The OECD principles cover organizational, technical, and scientific issues similar to those described in the U.S. regulations. The OECD Expert Group is now dealing with procedures for compliance with the principles and examining the relationships with the work on testing guidelines of other OECD Expert Groups in the Chemicals Programme.

It has been proposed that the OECD Council adopt the principle that data generated in one country, in accordance with the OECD Test Guidelines and the OECD Principles of Good Laboratory Practice, should be accepted in the other OECD countries.

TESTING REQUIREMENTS

In principle, the regulatory choices for prescribing tests on new substances fall into four broad groupings: (a) to require filing of data on health and environmental effects as part of the notification process, leaving the actual choice of test data to the manufacturer; (b) to require a base set of test data (subject to omissions, substitutions, and additions), leaving additional testing to the discretion of the manufacturer; (c) to require a base set and, at the same time, to prescribe criteria (for example, the tier-testing criteria mentioned earlier) by which additional test data may be required at a later time; or (d) to require a well-defined, complete set of test data, in each submission. The most recent EPA proposal for premanufacture notification requirements has adopted (a); the approach of 79/831/EEC is along the lines of (c). However, there are, within the flexibilities provided by each of these, many opportunities to create mutually compatible approaches.

OECD Expert Groups on testing have proposed two principles on the degree of flexibility that is appropriate in determining what tests should be performed:

- those conducting the tests must have the option to omit or substitute tests so long as they can scientifically justify their action and demonstrate the equal or superior performance and predictive power of replacement tests;

- those undertaking the assessments must have the option at any time to require additions or substitutions beyond the prescribed "information packages" in individual cases, so long as they can justify their course of action.

While lack of predictability of precise test requirements would at first appear to be an obstacle to international agreement, some degree of flexibility may actually allow agreement where it might not otherwise take place. For example, 79/831/EEC states that if a Member State is not satisfied with the information submitted or thinks a chemical may pose a danger, it can request further information, thus in principle establishing a basis for harmonization with the United States in instances where testing rules under TSCA require more information than is called for by 79/831/EEC. A provision permitting some flexibility in a prescribed scheme may allow people to agree to things that they might not agree to in its absence.

The authority to prescribe test requirements for all new chemical substances is not explicitly defined under TSCA, as it is under 79/831/EEC. EPA has no authority to require that all new chemical substances undergo a base set of tests, the results of which are to be submitted as a requirement of premanufacture notification (PMN). However, the agency is not prevented from providing guidance on the test data it considers adequate, and it has stated that it intends to establish such guidance. It has received proposals on appropriate guidelines from The Conservation Foundation[23] and others. EPA has supported the OECD minimum set of data and plans to issue the MPD as recommended testing for new chemicals.[24]

EPA does have the authority to require, by rule, testing of specific chemicals and categories of chemicals, and for these the agency has recently proposed generic test standards for health effects, including tests for acute and chronic animal toxicity. Generic test standards will, if made final, be employed by the agency as a basis for prescribing tests to be performed by a manufacturer or importer for those existing or new substances that are the subject of a testing rule. These standards should be consistent with OECD test guidelines that the U.S. agrees to adopt, though the test standards (which will apply only for those substances for which there is a testing rule) may be more specific than the OECD guidelines.

COST SHARING

Under 79/831/EEC, after September 18, 1981, each new marketer of a chemical is required to submit a dossier of information, unless the chemical is on an inventory of "old" chemicals. (No marketer is required to test an inventoried chemical under the EC Directive, though such requirements may appear in other directives or in the national laws of the EC Member States.) By requiring a separate dossier from each marketer, 79/831/EEC avoids the need for governments to address the question of how testing costs should be shared among notifiers. Negotiations can occur between notifiers, with later notifiers approaching earlier ones for permission, at a price, to use test data that have already been developed. Where negotiations fail to occur or break down, there may be some otherwise unnecessary duplicative testing of essentially identical substances. There are details to be worked out, such as how subsequent notifiers will learn the identity of earlier notifiers so that negotiations can be initiated, but the principle is straightforward: each notifier "owns" its own data; subject to a 10-year limit, others must buy the right to use the data or develop their own data for purposes of notification. This "ownership" in the EC depends on nondisclosure of the data by governments and by the company, but other devices could achieve the same purpose, such as affidavits of origin of the data coupled with international agreement on the need for permission from the originator of the data before others could use the information for purposes of notification.

Under TSCA, where only the first manufacturer or importer of a new substance is required to submit a dossier, the burden of notification cost, including the cost of testing, falls squarely on the innovator (unless there is a general testing rule in force for the substance, in which event certain provisions, discussed below, for sharing of testing costs apply). Since subsequent manufacturers and importers are not required to notify, they have no incentive to pay the first notifier anything for test data submitted with a new chemical notice.

TSCA also provides for the testing of old chemicals, and EPA has the authority to designate who shall test as well as who shall pay. In principle, producers could get together and undertake testing on a common basis, or one could do the testing and be reimbursed by the others.

Some very difficult questions arise if decisions on cost sharing for tests on old chemicals are to be made by EPA. Should costs be borne by manufacturers only, or should processors (those who use chemicals in their products, but do not themselves manufacture the chemicals) be included? Should all manufacturers and processors share, no matter where the risk of the chemical is presumed to come from? If the risk is only associated with manufacturing, should the processors also share in the testing? There are a whole series of such issues that remain to be resolved.

A still different approach could involve the funding by governments of national testing programs or international testing programs with worldwide participation and worldwide involvement, using the best laboratories in each specialized area of interest. Such funding might be used to pay for testing of chemicals of special concern such as those that are pervasive in the environment. This approach does not internalize testing costs into the cost of producing the chemicals. Therefore, unless elaborate schemes are devised that allocate costs back to industry (for example, by taxation or by fees), this approach is tantamount to making the taxpayer provide for the necessary testing.

The problem of determining how the costs for testing of old chemicals should be shared has three components—a legal component, an equity component, and a practical component. The legal component can be solved by granting government authorities the power to require full investigation of a chemical by any producer or importer of that chemical. The fact that the power is there can be helpful whether or not it is actually used.

Administrators, to whom power is delegated, need to consider issues of equity among parties. Of course, this problem can be avoided if industrial organizations handle the problem on their own initiative. Moreover, the chemical industry has organizations that may be able to resolve such matters among their members. For example, the Chemical Manufacturers Association in the United States has proposed that allocation of testing costs be based on production volume and be determined by the involved industries whenever possible.[25]

As a practical matter, it would seem that problems of cost sharing do not provide convincing reason to deter any government from an intent to have appropriate studies carried out. The legal, equity, and practical problems can be solved.

TESTING COSTS

How the base set established by 79/831/EEC will work, how often the escape clauses will be opened to exempt chemicals from testing, and how many will go through the entire gamut of testing are all open questions. This important point has been discussed in Europe, though no firm conclusions have been reached. Only practice will tell. But many anticipate that the majority of the new substances for which notification is required and which are marketed in volumes over one ton will be tested fully at the base set level, and that escape provisions will be used rather selectively.

The principal determinants of cost are the details of the test protocols, for example, how many animals will be used in a test, the extent of study of tissues for pathology, and so on. Scientists may insist on having as much information as possible and may insist on protocols that are very expensive. From a public policy point of view, one looks for an optimum testing requirement that takes into account competing demands and the need to test many different chemicals. From a corporate strategy point of view, a number of chemicals may be subjected to preliminary tests, in some instances, before one chemical is chosen for commercialization.

Economic distortions increase as testing costs are raised. Base-set requirements have been considered in terms of what can be done within fixed-price ceilings and the resultant costs have then been compared with other research costs. It is, in part, on this basis that figures of about $10,000 to $50,000 are frequently discussed, since higher figures are generally considered to be beyond the economic capability of industry for most new developments. The cost of testing at the full EC base-set level is generally estimated to be in this $10,000 to $50,000 range.

One can also make a distinction between new chemicals that are going to involve the construction of a new plant and new chemicals that are going to be made with existing equipment. Only a small percentage of the overall number of new chemicals is likely to fall into the first of these categories, but, for these, testing costs will usually be only a very small percentage of the initial investment. At least for American industry, the cost of constructing a plant to produce a major new chemical could be $20 to $60 million.[26] Under these circumstances, $50,000 or even ten times that in testing costs is not going to make much of an impact on the decision to proceed.

If one assumes $50,000 for testing each of, say, 400 to 1,000 new chemicals per year, the resulting cost of $20 to $50 million is still insignificant compared to the total research budget of the chemical industry. But, for certain products or certain chemicals, such expenditures may be a significant barrier to commercialization, particularly for new chemicals of small volume, those priced relatively low, or with low profitability. One of the reasons why the United States has not committed itself to a base set is because of concern regarding the effect of notification and testing on these low-volume, low-price, or low-profitability chemicals. The problems of the small manufacturer have been in the forefront of these discussions.

One can ask whether development of a chemical is worthwhile if the manufacturer cannot afford to test it, or whether low-volume chemicals should be exempted from testing. This kind of debate leads nowhere until it is recast into politically acceptable terms, since exemptions from testing for some new chemicals (low-volume chemicals, in particular) can have a substantial impact on the testing cost that is perceived as acceptable for other new chemicals. Some kind of volume exemption—such as the one-ton EC exemption—is likely to be politically, economically, and administratively inseparable from a base-set testing requirement. On these counts, one can speculate that exemptions from testing requirements in the EC (for polymers and nonmarketed intermediates—as discussed in Chapter IV) must also have significantly increased the acceptability of a base set to industry in the EC.

Such hard choices have not been made as yet in the United States, which has the option of setting such rules or operating on a more *ad hoc* case-by-case basis. The latter approach obviously would pose questions, since it would, for a long time, be difficult to judge what the U.S. standards really are, and whether they are being applied in a manner consistent with the purposes of TSCA.

Of course, if extensive testing is already being done by industry, then the incremental cost of testing new chemicals under these new laws is smaller than would otherwise be inferred. The general statement has been made periodically that most of the tests in the EC base set are normally performed by U.S. industry.[27] The early experience under TSCA is grossly at variance with this claim.[28] It is true that some of the early new chemical notices under TSCA are for substances that would not require notification in the EC, and others would be exempted from testing until placed on the market in larger than one-ton quantities. Nevertheless, while the number of notices is increasing, the paucity of testing, in comparison with the EC base set, is becoming increasingly evident. Of course, these early TSCA notices may not be a fair sample of what will happen later.

It is, in fact, likely that there is no single "chemical industry" and that the industry that develops new chemicals is highly diverse in the nature of its products and in the testing it routinely performs on its own initiative. Among the base-set tests, the sub-chronic toxicity test is by far the single most costly element. It is for this reason that many of the discussions of base-set testing have centered on the sub-chronic test and the choice of protocol for it—since the details of the test substantially influence its cost.

Finally, the economic impact of a regulatory scheme includes many other considerations besides testing costs. Regulatory response, innovation impedence, administrative costs, and a full range of other factors need to be taken into account.

Chapter IV
Notification Requirements

In many parts of the world, some chemical products, particularly drugs or pesticides that contain chemicals intended to be biologically active, have long been controlled by explicit registration requirements in which government approval is needed before a manufacturer puts the product on the market. In contrast, TSCA, 79/831/EEC, and other recent laws, while requiring the submission of information in a notification, do not require approval of a new chemical before manufacture or marketing can commence.

The information contained in notifications is of several general kinds. It includes:

- The identity of the chemical;
- When the new chemical is to be manufactured, marketed, or imported;
- Who will manufacture, market, or import the chemical;
- Exposure information;
- Hazard information.

Exposure assessment must consider some or all of the following factors: the processes by which a chemical is manufactured, its uses and methods of disposal, its fate in the environment (including its tendency to persist, or degrade, under actual conditions of use and disposal), its physicochemical characteristics, as well as the nature of its interactions with living organisms (such as its tendencies to accumulate in tissue). The present state of the art of exposure assessment frequently requires that extensive assumptions be made about many of these factors.

Hazard assessment requires an understanding of a chemical's effects on living organisms and ecosystems, especially its toxic effects on man or other species that may be at risk due to exposure to the chemical, as well as the dynamics of a chemical's uptake from the environment, the effects caused by its interactions with other chemicals, and the hazards presented by other chemicals into which it may be transformed by environmental processes. Complete information about hazards will never be available, and much of the information that is may relate only more or less directly to actual hazards, since it is usually only surrogate information, for example, laboratory test results rather than actual extensive field studies. Some of the best toxicological tests are also the most time consuming and most costly; hence, other tests of lesser certainty will sometimes be appropriate— taking cost, time, and risk into account.

Given all of these complexities, neither government nor industry will have a complete dossier on a chemical. Some initial package of information is nonetheless needed, as well as an understanding that new information for the dossier may be required from time to time or as particular reasons emerge for concern about the chemical.

The requirement that there be an initial package of information is common to TSCA and 79/831/EEC. Both specify that certain information must be submitted; yet they also differ in important respects. The similarities and differences between TSCA and 79/831/EEC define the major issues to be discussed in this chapter. At the outset, it is important to note the transformation of goals and objectives brought about by a notification requirement. While the underlying goal is to regulate development and commercial use of chemicals so that certain risks can be controlled, both TSCA and 79/831/EEC actually function first by regulating the development and use of information.

PREMARKET VS. PREMANUFACTURE NOTIFICATION

TSCA is a system for *premanufacture* notification, while 79/831/EEC is a system for *premarketing* notification. This is an important distinction. Under TSCA, for example, notification is required for substances used as intermediates, that is, as substances that corporations isolate and use for commercial purposes but do not place on the market. These substances, when they are not placed on the market, would not require notification under 79/831/EEC. (The difference may not in practice be as great as it appears; the view has been expressed that substances that are in any way transferred, say, from one division of a corporation to another, with internal corporate book payments for these deliveries, may be considered to have been placed on the market.)

The choice of premanufacture (as in the United States) vs. premarket (as in the EC) notification probably reflects differences in the opportunities governments have under other statutes to control chemicals that are manufactured but not marketed, and also differences of emphasis on intertional trade. The U.S. premanufacture notification requirements apply to imported substances, because TSCA includes importation within its definition of "to manufacture." From the point of view of new chemical notification by an importer of chemical substances, a premanufacture system is indistinguishable from a premarketing one (except if there are instances where importation is not construed as placing on the market).

SUBSTANCES REQUIRING NOTIFICATION

Determining what qualifies as a substance requiring notification may be a complicated process. Among the points to be considered are the form—substance, mixture, preparation, or article; its relation to an inventory; and specific exemptions or exclusions. There are significant differences between TSCA and 79/831/EEC in each of these areas.

Chemical Substances, Mixtures, Preparations, and Articles

Chemical substances are defined in very broad terms under 79/831/EEC and TSCA.

- The Directive 79/831/EEC defines substances as "chemical elements and their compounds as they occur in the natural state or as produced by industry, including any additives required for the purpose of placing them on the market."

- Under the U.S. law, a chemical substance means "any organic or inorganic substance of a particular molecular identity, including any combination of such substances occurring in whole or in part as a result of a chemical reaction or occurring in nature, and any chemical element or uncombined radical . . . ."

Both definitions are broader than what a chemist would use to define a specific chemical. The U.S. definition unambiguously includes combinations of chemicals, and the EC definition seems to do so also. These definitions, though in some respects a chemical fiction, are useful, since they would appear to allow many commonly used materials (such as the natural oils and waxes) to be dealt with as whole compositions rather than separately in terms of each of their complex constituents. Although the two definitions differ and are complex, they may in practice come to have similar or identical meanings.

A chemical substance may occur as part of a mixture under TSCA. A mixture, as defined, is a combination (of two or more chemical substances) that is not the result of a chemical reaction and does not occur in nature (reaction products are considered to be mixtures, however, if the final combination could have been prepared by mixing commercially available substances). Under 79/831/EEC, a preparation is defined as a mixture or solution comprised of two or more substances. Thus, paints would be mixtures under TSCA and preparations under 79/831/EEC.

An article, as defined by the TSCA Inventory Regulations, is a product manufactured in a particular shape, which does not change chemical composition in use, except to the extent needed to accomplish the article's purpose—as in, for example, the chemical changes during development of photographic film. A fluid is never an article, since it has no fixed shape. The Directive 79/831/EEC does not discuss articles.

Notification is not required for mixtures or preparations, but is required for new substances in mixtures (U.S.) or in preparations (EC). Notification is also required in the United States for new substances in domestically manufactured articles. The difficulties that articles pose internationally are discussed in detail in Chapter VI.

Some commercial chemicals have a known, definite structure. Benzene and methyl alcohol are examples. Others are of unknown or variable structure. Linseed oil, casein, and coal tar are examples of substances defined in the United States as UVCB substances (Chemical Substances of Unknown or Variable Composition, Complex Reaction Products, and Biological Materials). Notification is required in the United States for new UVCB substances as well as for new substances of known, definite composition. Presumably, this will also be the case in the European Community.

A certain degree of arbitrariness necessarily intrudes in the definition of UVCB substances. To illustrate, each of the following is listed as a separate "chemical substance" in the U.S. Initial Inventory:

sulfite liquor: black, vanillin
sulfite liquor: spent
sulfite liquor: spent, alkali treated
sulfite liquor: spent, copper complex
sulfite liquor: spent, fermented
sulfite liquor: spent, manganese complex
sulfite liquor: spent, oxidixed, insoluble sediment
sulfite liquor: spent, sulfur dioxide treated

There is no reason in principle for all of these separate listings; they could have been combined into larger categories. One entry called "sulfite liquor" might have been chosen to encompass them. With firm intent, a substantial degree of harmonization of such complex definitions can be achieved. Otherwise, it is quite possible for differences to develop of the most mischievous kind; for example, chemicals that are modifications of one structural theme could be considered one substance by one trading partner and many substances (each requiring separate notification) by another.

Role of the Inventory

Both 79/831/EEC and TSCA provide for inventories of chemical substances. In the United States, notification does not have to be given for substances appearing on the inventory. Similarly, substances on an EC inventory would not need notification in the Community. In either case, inscription of a substance on an inventory has the practical effect of making it an "old" substance.

The initial U.S. TSCA inventory, published in 1979, listed about 45,000 chemical substances and categories of substances manufactured and/or imported for commercial purposes since January 1, 1975. The inventory was compiled from reports by manufacturers and importers under regulations[1] issued in 1977. A revised inventory will include additional reports from importers of mixtures and from processors. Since July 1979, after the initial inventory was published, any domestic manufacturer or importer of a chemical substance not on the inventory has been required to submit a premanufacture notification. (Importers of mixtures and processors will be subject to premanufacturing notification rules after the revised inventory is completed.)

The TSCA inventory is dynamic and may be changed in several ways:

- A chemical substance will be added to the inventory when actual manufacture or importation occurs. This may not happen till well after expiration of its "new chemical" notification period. (Such changes will occur regularly as a matter of course.)

- The inventory may not include all reportable substances, since importers of articles are not required to report the substances they import as part of those articles. (EPA has not explicitly excluded the possibility of future reporting requirements for such materials, though it is recognized that the practical problems are immense for across-the-board action of this type.)

- Exemptions as currently defined may be changed. (Changes of this kind are not likely to occur often, if at all.)

- The description of UVCB substances or other chemicals grouped together as a "chemical substance" on the inventory may be revised so as either to increase or decrease the number of substances inscribed on the inventory. (This may become important as inventory entries are reviewed in the context of testing requirements and control actions.)

In 79/831/EEC, the definition of a substance requiring notification is not formally linked, as it is under TSCA, to the existence of an inventory. Hence, 79/831/EEC can be made operative even if there is no Community inventory (though it appears likely that an inventory will be prepared). A chemical marketed by a company for the first time after September 18, 1981, would need to be treated as a new substance, with notification required, even if the same chemical had been marketed earlier by another company. If an inventory is prepared, substances appearing on the inventory would become exempt from new chemical notification.

The EC inventory would comprise a list of chemicals on the market on September 18, 1981. Thus, the EC inventory will be static in the sense that no substance marketed for the first time after September 18, 1981, will ever be added to the inventory; hence, each new marketer of a post-September 18, 1981, substance must separately present a new chemical notification. (Notification requirements are scaled down for those who start to market a substance more than 10 years after its first notification.)

New Substances

To review briefly, in the EC a substance placed on the market for the first time after September 18, 1981, is new and remains new. In the United States, any chemical substance not on the inventory is a new substance. It becomes an "old" substance after notification is given by one manufacturer or importer. The chemical is placed on the inventory when it is actually manufactured or imported. One consequence of these differences is that only the first manufacturer or importer of a new substance notifies in the United States, while the first and all subsequent manufacturers of a substance marketed after September 18, 1981, must notify in the European Community.

The U.S. law also provides for notification of "significant new uses," though the term has not as yet been defined by EPA. This kind of notification may be used as a follow-up mechanism for new chemicals, but it also may be used for "old" chemicals. In the EC, as discussed in the previous chapter and below, follow-up information is required as the amount of a substance placed on the market increases past certain benchmark figures.

Imports

Both TSCA and 79/831/EEC cover imports. In the EC, placing a substance on the market means supplying or making it available to third parties. A substance is considered to be placed on the market when it is imported into the EC customs territory. In the United States, the term "manufacture" means to produce, manufacture, or to import into the U.S. customs territory. The two systems are indistinguishable to the importer; in either case, the time of importation is decisive in defining the requirement for notification.

Exemptions and Exclusions

Neither TSCA nor 79/831/EEC applies to certain classes of substances (such as drugs, foods, and pesticides) already covered by other legislation. Beyond these exclusions, TSCA regulations[2] require notification for all new commercial chemicals, with the following complex group of exceptions:

- Substances used only for research and development, manufactured or imported only in quantities needed for that purpose, and used under the supervision of a technically qualified person;

- Substances used solely for test marketing if the manufacturer or importer can show they will not present an unreasonable risk;

- Impurities, that is, chemicals not intentionally present;

- By-products or co-products having no commercial purpose (or only a limited purpose specifically related to use as a fuel, a landfill, a soil enricher, or a source of valuable extractable components—for example, waste gaseous hydrocarbons used as a fuel and produced incidental to manufacture of chemicals for commercial use);

- Nonisolated intermediates, that is, substances consumed in whole or in part in chemical reactions used to manufacture another substance, or used to alter the rate of chemical reactions, and not intentionally removed from the manufacturing equipment;

- Substances produced incidental to the use of other substances, as follows (this is a complicated group of exceptions presented here for purposes of completeness): substances produced by reactions that occur incidental to exposure, such as the partial oxidation products of paints; substances that result from reactions during storage, such as the decomposition products of antioxidant additives; substances produced during end use of other chemicals in articles, such as matches, photographic film, and batteries; and substances that form upon use of inks, curable molding compounds, or other substances formed during the manufacture of an article destined for the market without further chemical changes (except for changes noted above which themselves lead to exempted substances).

Under 79/831/EEC, substances used for research or analysis are to be considered as having been notified within the meaning of the Directive insofar as they are placed on the market:

- for the purpose of determining their properties in accordance with the Directive, that is, for testing;
- in quantities of less than one ton per year per manufacturer or importer for research or analysis purposes and intended solely for laboratories.

The Directive 79/831/EEC also specifies that a substance placed on the market at the research and development stage (with a limited number of registered customers, in quantities limited to the purpose of research and development but amounting to more than one ton per year per manufacturer) shall qualify for exemption for a period of one year; this exemption is subject to the caveat that the manufacturer must announce identity, labeling data, and quantity to the competent authorities of each Member State where the manufacture, research, or development takes place and must comply with any conditions imposed by those authorities on such research and development. (Full notification under the Directive only needs to be addressed to the Member State where the substance is first placed on the market.) The manufacturer must also give an assurance that the substance or the preparation in which it is incorporated will be handled only by the customer's staff, will be used under controlled conditions, and will not be made available to the public. This amounts to a limited kind of notification. After the one-year period, or whenever any of the other conditions ceases to apply, these substances are subject to full notification requirements.

Substances placed on the market in quantities less than one ton per year per manufacturer or importer are considered as having been notified in the EC even if used for other than research and analysis purposes, providing the manufacturer announces their identity, labeling data, and quantities to the competent authorities of the Member States where the substances are placed on the market, and complies with any conditions imposed by those authorities. This, too, is a limited kind of notification. Full notification is required when any manufacturer or importer exceeds the one-ton limit.

The handling of small-volume chemicals thus differs in the United States and the European Community. In the EC, a value judgment is implicitly made that a lesser degree of notification is required for chemicals produced at less than one ton per manufacturer per year, and that there should be a partial or complete exemption from notification requirements for substances used in analysis, research, and development. The U.S. law provides a more general exemption for substances used solely for research and development, but does not address limitations of notification for low-volume chemicals.

The EC Directive does not call for notification of polymers (polymerizates, polycondensates, and polyadducts) except those containing in combined form 2 percent or more of any monomer unmarketed before September 18, 1981. (Polymers are usually synthesized from monomers. In general, monomers are small molecules, many of which—commonly hundreds, thousands, or more—must be linked together chemically to form a polymer.) Thus, polymers not based substantially on new monomers are exempted from notification. There is no comparable exemption in the United States.

Many polymers have such large molecular size that they are not readily absorbed upon skin contact. Thus many polymers—not necessarily all—are relatively innocuous in use. One can infer from the EC exemption that a value judgment is being made to the effect that polymers as a class are likely to be less hazardous than other chemicals, and that the cost of notification would be high in relation to the relatively small likelihood of significant risk. While there may be significant hazards associated with some polymers of very low molecular weight or those that are respirable dusts, the exemption does illustrate how certain substances or conditions of presumed low risk may be singled out for special treatment, with the intent of making the overall system more cost-effective.

CONTENT OF NOTICES

The goal of new chemical notification is to supply the information needed to assess risks of injury to man and the environment. There is some agreement on the key types of information needed for risk assessment. These include the identity of the chemical, its physicochemical characteristics, toxicity studies, and volume and use data. The differences between the Community and U.S. approaches are in the specificity and kinds of information requirements.

It is difficult to state, in the abstract, whether one system or another is preferable. In both instances, the implementation procedure must be taken into account. TSCA is framed with a national administration and a complex, public policymaking system in mind. A certain degree of ambiguity in the notice requirements may thus be acceptable. In contrast, the requirements of 79/831/EEC appear to be quite specific. This approach is typical of the needs of the Community at its present stage, where marketing of a chemical throughout the Community can occur after review of a notice by only one Member State, thus, it is desirable to achieve as much precision as possible in the Community Directive. In all likelihood, any other international system of notification involving mutual recognition will need to achieve a comparable degree of precision.

The European Community

The EC Directive prescribes that the technical dossier should contain at least the information and the results of a series of studies described in Annex VII of the Directive (subject to escape clauses), as follows:

- the identity of the substance, that is, its chemical name, empirical and structural formula, and composition, including impurities;
- information relating to proposed uses and estimated production and/or imports for each of the anticipated uses or fields of application;
- physicochemical properties of the substance, for example, melting point, boiling point, relative density, and so on;
- results of a series of tests, including assessment of acute effects, of irritant or corrosive effects on the skin and eyes, sensitization tests, mutagenicity tests, and a test for sub-acute toxicity;
- results of ecotoxicological studies, including acute effects on fish and acute effects on daphnia, as well as certain tests for degradation;
- the possibilities of rendering the substance harmless.

In addition to presenting the technical dossier, the notifier must present the competent authority with a declaration concerning the unfavorable effects of the new substance in terms of the various uses envisaged, and a proposal for the classification and labeling of the new substance in accordance with the Directive. The notifier also has to make proposals to the competent authority for any measures relating to the conditions recommended to limit unfavorable effects.

The United States

Each manufacturer or importer who submits a new chemical notice under TSCA must include certain kinds of information, and is encouraged to submit additional information.

The following types of information are required by TSCA:

- a description of the new chemical substance, its chemical identity, molecular structure, and common or trade name;
- the proposed categories of use;
- the estimated total amount to be manufactured or processed;
- the estimated amount to be manufactured and processed for each proposed category of use;

- a description of the by-products resulting from manufacture, processing, use, or disposal;

- the number of individuals expected to be exposed in their place of employment and estimates of the expected duration of exposure;

- manner and methods of disposal;

- test data in the possession or control of the notifier related to the effects on health or the environment of any manufacturing, processing, distribution in commerce, use, or disposal of the substance, or any article containing the substance; and

- other data concerning health and environmental effects, insofar as known to the notifier or reasonably ascertainable.

EPA has elaborated on the details of these requirements of TSCA and has proposed forms and regulations for use in premanufacturing notifications.[3] These additional documents describe in detail what must be submitted as well as optional information the agency would like to receive.

Fixed vs. Flexible Requirements

Two approaches to initial requirements for notification have emerged. One emphasizes submission of all available data when the chemical is first manufactured or imported. The other fixes specific requirements for initial notification, and additional requirements as use of the chemical grows. TSCA has been described as taking the first approach and the EC Directive the second.

An argument for the first approach is that it is important for the government to know as much as is known about the risks presented by the chemical substance so that risk can be evaluated on as informed a basis as possible. The argument for the second approach is that priorities must be set. The concept of "step sequence" testing uses the second approach, as discussed in Chapter III (Assessing Hazard).

As implementation of TSCA evolves, it is not at all clear that information submitted in new chemical notices will actually be as extensive as required in the EC. Early experience with the U.S. system indicates that very little testing is being done in most instances.[4] In fact, there may be an incentive not to test, since any data known to the notifier—including data that reveal hazard—must be submitted.

While 79/831/EEC appears to have fixed requirements for a base set, the requirements need not be satisfied "if it is not technically possible or if it does not appear necessary to give information," providing the reasons are stated. The extent to which this clause will be used to escape testing requirements is not yet evident. A burden is placed on the notifier to show why it is either not technically possible or not necessary to provide the information.

Since notification may be made in any of the EC Member States, it remains to be determined how criteria for these provisions will be defined and standardized throughout the Community. Furthermore, there are ambiguities about what will happen if a manufacturer has additional data. If a company has done a cancer study but the EC notification only requires consideration of the need for acute studies and sub-chronic studies, nothing would bar the company from sending the cancer study to the competent authority and nothing would bar the competent authority from asking for it. The sense of the Directive would appear to be that the information should be supplied, but as currently written it is not a very precisely stated obligation. In practice, the information may be supplied in accordance with general provisions of national administrative procedures rather than because of explicit legal prescriptions in the national laws implementing 79/831/EEC. In France, for example, it has so far been no problem for the government to obtain the results of all tests performed by a company.[5]

In the EC, notifiers of substances for which there has already been notification are required to submit "new knowledge of the effects of the substance on man and/or the environment of which he may reasonably be expected to have become aware." If a study is known to the notifier, he must submit the study. Thus, "reasonably ascertainable," which are words used in TSCA, may have their European equivalent in the statement "of which he might reasonably be expected to become aware." Though these differences of wording would not appear to pose a major problem, there are specific questions not yet resolved that need attention. For example, "reasonably ascertainable" in the United States may include an obligation to review the literature and provide literature references to EPA. Related to this is the U.S. requirement that information be submitted if it is in the "possession and control of the notifier." The concept of possession and control raises a number of questions—for example, for multinational corporations, is it the obligation of a parent corporation or one member of a family of related subsidiaries to obtain data from other affiliated corporations?

Differences of these sorts will not be settled by comparisons of TSCA and 79/831/EEC. It is not surprising that TSCA and the implementing regulations now being developed by EPA raise detailed questions that are difficult to assess vis-a-vis the Community approach. The EC Directive must itself be transformed into national laws in which the more exact obligations of notifiers may be specified. Though actual practices that will evolve under these two systems are in many ways not clear, there are many more options and opportunities for harmonization than are evident at first examination.

WHO MUST NOTIFY

Notification requirements in the EC apply not only the first time a substance is placed on the market but each time a different manufacturer or importer places that substance on the market. The Directive aims, therefore, by means of the notification system, to provide for the continuing surveillance of chemicals in the environment. In addition, this feature of the Directive takes into account the practical fact that products manufactured by different companies may use different processes, and may contain different minor components and impurities. In this sense, the EC Directive provides for more complete tracking than does TSCA of different products known in commerce by the same name.

Since only the first manufacturer or importer of a substance notifies under the TSCA notification system, no subsequent manufacturer is required to test or to reimburse the first manufacturer (unless, as noted earlier, there is a special testing rule that applies to the notified substance). One purpose of this approach is to conserve testing resources by eliminating duplicative testing requirements. A consequence, however, may be that companies will lose some of their incentive to innovate, since only the first notifier is required to bear the cost of testing.

Notification does not provide for automatic follow-up of new chemicals under TSCA. General reporting rules and "significant new use" rules are used instead, as discussed elsewhere in this chapter.

Importers must notify under TSCA in the United States and under 79/831/EEC in the European Community. Notification is not at present required for substances imported as part of articles because of the practical problems of dealing with this issue (see Chapter VI).

Exporters from the Community need not notify under 79/831/EEC; the reach of the Directive applies only to substances placed on the market in Member States. TSCA may be interpreted as giving EPA authority to require testing of substances intended for export, and authority to control those that will present an unreasonable domestic risk in, for instance, manufacture and transport. In addition, companies must inform EPA of their interest to export substances that are subject to TSCA rules or orders, including test rules and controls that limit or ban domestic use.

The costs of notification have been of particular concern to small companies.[6] Presumably, exemptions for substances with annual production under one ton will reduce the testing burden of notification in the EC for some small companies, although small businesses do not necessarily develop small-volume chemicals. Under the TSCA inventory regulations,[7] EPA used a $5 million sales cutoff to define a small company. Small companies receive special consideration under some TSCA reporting requirements but are not exempt from giving notification of new substances.

Companies that incorporate chemicals into products, but do not themselves manufacture the chemicals, are called processors in the United States. These companies may decide, for example, which chemicals will be used in a coating for a water pipe or to treat a fabric. Processors often have essential information on human and environmental exposure. The United States requires manufacturers rather than processors to submit new chemical notifications; yet manufacturers frequently do not know the uses to which their products will be put by the processors. Whether manufacturers will be required to contact customers to obtain information for premanufacture notification of new chemicals is under consideration by EPA,[8] but is complicated by the secrecy that surrounds information on specific uses of chemicals. The issue has been extensively debated in the United States and has not yet been resolved. EPA has the authority to require by rule a wide variety of information from processors as well as manufacturers and importers.

The Directive 79/831/EEC requires notification only by manufacturers and importers into the Community. Thus, notification is presumably not required of processors in the Community.

FOLLOW-UP NOTIFICATION

The introduction of a new commercial chemical may at the outset present little opportunity for risk to human health or the environment. For example, the substance may be made in small amounts, and it may be used in a way that exposes few people, none to a significant degree. Over time, as more uses are discovered and larger quantities are made, more significant levels of risk may develop. The initial notification informs the government of the intent to manufacture or market a chemical, but governments also need to keep track of chemicals as new uses develop and the nature and magnitude of the risk changes. Follow-up mechanisms serve this purpose.

As with new chemical notifications, there is a major difference between the EC and U.S. approaches to follow-up—namely, explicit and specific steps are called for in the Community Directive as compared with broad, yet relatively flexible opportunities for follow-up under TSCA.

The European Community

Under 79/831/EEC, there is an obligation to provide quantitative and qualitative information about chemical substances when they are to be placed on the market and at several stages thereafter. The base set as adopted by the Council provides the basic safety net. Beyond that, there is a step-sequence plan (*Stufenplan*) that links additional testing requirements to the quantities of a particular chemical put into circulation by a manufacturer or importer and to the results of earlier tests. The Directive 79/831/EEC might possibly allow a dangerous chemical product to find its way onto the market. But, even if this did happen, the hope and expectation is that the checks at different production levels contained in the step-sequence plan would enable a disaster or even any extensive difficulty to be averted in good time.

Under 79/831/EEC, any notifier of a substance would be required to inform the competent authority, as prescribed by the Directive, of: changes in the annual or total quantities placed on the market; new knowledge of the effects of the substance on man and/or the environment; new uses for which the substance is placed on the market; and changes in the composition of the substance that might result from modifications of the manufacturing process.

Extending the notification requirement beyond the base set was intensively discussed during the development of 79/831/EEC. As finally agreed on by the Council of the EC, the system contains two levels beyond the base set. At Level 1, when the quantity of a substance placed on the market by a notifier reaches a level of 10 tons per year or a cumulative total of 50 tons (and in certain circumstances before Level 1), the competent authority may require certain additional studies taking into account:

- current knowledge of the substance;
- known and planned uses; and
- the results of the tests carried out in the context of the base set.

The additional tests at Level 1 may include toxicological studies of fertility, teratology, more prolonged sub-chronic/chronic toxicity, additional mutagenesis studies, and a variety of ecotoxicological tests for toxicity to various plant and and animal species, as well as biodegradation and accumulation studies. Many of these tests are described in 79/831/EEC in a manner that emphasizes scientific judgment based on the results of earlier tests. For example, a ninety-day to two-year further investigation of chronic effects is called for if the results of the sub-acute study in the base set, or other relevant information, demonstrate the need for further investigation; some examples of relevant effects calling for further study are cited directly in 79/831/EEC, thus providing specific, illustrative guidance.

The Directive specifies that, in any case, the notifier shall inform the competent authority if the quantity of a substance placed on the market reaches a level of 100 tons per year or a cumulative total of 500 tons. On receipt of such information, the competent authority shall require Level 1 tests to be carried out unless in any particular case an alternative scientific study would be preferable.

The process is triggered a second time—Level 2 beyond the base level—when the quantity of a substance placed on the market by a notifier reaches 1,000 tons per year or a total of 5,000 tons. At this point, the notifier informs the competent authority, and the latter draws up a program of tests to be carried out by the notifier so that the risks of the substance for man and the environment can be evaluated.

The Level 2 tests cover the following, unless there are strong reasons supported by evidence that this program should not be followed:

- Toxicological studies: chronic toxicity study; carcinogenicity study; fertility study; teratology study; acute and sub-acute toxicity studies on second species; and additional toxicokinetic studies.

- Ecotoxicological studies: additional tests for accumulation, degradation, and mobility; prolonged toxicity study with fish; additional toxicity study with birds and other organisms, and an absorption-desorption study.

In some instances, 79/831/EEC states the circumstances that should lead to performance of these more extensive tests. In many instances, the need to conduct the tests is contingent on Level 1 results or other kinds of information already in hand. Thus, at Level 2 there also appears to be an attempt to provide specific guidance, tempered by the need for flexibility.

The United States

In the U.S. system, once there is notification and manufacture of a new chemical, it becomes an old chemical. It may be made subject to rules requiring additional information and/or notification, but there is no automatic schedule as in 79/831/EEC.

For example, under TSCA, substances produced in volumes under one ton require notification in the same manner as larger-volume substances. Once manufactured, all substances become old chemicals and are entered on the inventory; others can manufacture or import these substances without informing EPA, unless EPA decides to use some other provisions of TSCA to obtain this information. There is no automatic procedure to inform EPA that the chemical is produced in different amounts at some time after the initial notification.

One way of dealing with this problem would be for EPA to adopt base-set testing guidelines for new substances expected to be manufactured or imported at quantities greater than one ton per year. There could be follow-up for every chemical under one ton for which a lesser degree of testing was submitted. This could be accomplished by defining manufacture or importation in excess of one ton per year as a "significant new use" and requiring additional notification when this cut-off point is reached. (There are many possible variations on this theme. The cut-off point could, for example, be "placing one ton per year on the market.")

TSCA requires a determination "by rule" if the EPA Administrator wishes to require follow-up notification under the "significant new use" provisions of the Act. In making a determination, the Administrator must follow certain procedural rules and must consider all relevant factors, including the projected volume of manufacturing and processing of the substance, the extent to which the use changes the type or form of exposure of humans or the environment to the substance, the extent to which the use increases the magnitude and duration of exposure of humans or the environment to the substance, and the reasonably anticipated ways in which the substance will be manufactured, processed, distributed, and disposed of.

The manufacturer or processor must notify the Administrator at least 90 days before beginning to manufacture or process a chemical substance for a use that the EPA Administrator has determined is a "significant new use" of the substance. If a testing rule for the substance is in effect, the manufacturer must submit with his notice the test data required by the test rule. No "significant new use" rules have yet been issued, but such rules are being considered, particularly for follow-up to new chemical notifications.

TSCA provides EPA with fairly broad discretionary authority to require manufacturers and processors of chemicals to keep records and make reports. EPA is in the process of deciding just how these authorities should be used for following new chemicals. It is considering triggers for the submission of follow-up information for new chemicals and what this information should be. Clearly, approaches on which there is international agreement can have a major impact in this area.

REVIEW OF NOTICES BY GOVERNMENT

TSCA uses notification as an opportunity, although not the only one, to determine whether additional information is needed or whether controls are needed to prevent unreasonable risk of injury to health or the environment. The U.S. approach is sometimes confused with licensing or certification, since a risk assessment can be made on a chemical during the 90 days (extendable to 180 days) before it may be manufactured or imported, and EPA may act to delay, limit, or stop the proposed manufacture or importation. No positive approval of a notification is required, however, so calling the process licensing or certification is not really accurate. In the Community, a notification is reviewed by a competent national authority to ensure that the required information is submitted; the substance may be placed on the market 45 days later if the notification is complete and the chemical is proposed to be packaged and labeled in accord with the EC Directive. While 79/831/EEC does not require a risk assessment, some Member States appear to be preparing to perform them. However, most assessments can be expected to take more than the 45 days between notification and marketing.

The European Community

The Directive 79/831/EEC describes in some detail how information for notification is to be submitted and transferred within the Community. Notification takes place in the country of manufacture or, if the substance is imported from outside the Community, in the country into which it is first imported. A notification properly made in one Member State of the Community is valid in other Member States. In other words, a manufacturer or importer who has properly given notification for a substance in the country of origin or of first importation is free to put it on the market in other countries of the Community. Unless the authorities in the other countries invoke the safeguard clause, which enables them to restrict temporarily the entry of a substance they consider to be a hazard to health and safety, they are bound to accept that substance on the market. Thus, the Member State in which notification occurs in effect reviews the notice on behalf of all Member States.

The Directive is designed to remove barriers to trade within the Community, as well as to protect health and the environment. Because of the substitution of one single notification procedure for nine possibly very different notification procedures, a manufacturer may save much time and expense. He may safely project sales on a Community-wide basis without fear that in one or more countries of the Community his product will be blocked by capricious regulations concerning marketing.

When a Member State receives a notification dossier, it sends a copy of the dossier or a summary of it to the Commission of the European Community, together with any relevant comments. When further tests are required because of higher levels of production, the Member State need only send the Commission a statement of the tests chosen, the reasons for their choice, and an assessment of results. The Commission is to forward the notification dossier or the summary of it as well as other relevant information to the other Member States.

The other Member States may not be satisfied with the adequacy, completeness, or interpretation of the information forwarded by the Commission. Any Member State may, for these or other reasons, consult with the

Commission, or directly with the Member State that received the original notification, on specific details of the data contained in the dossier.

Each of the Member States may also suggest that further tests or information be requested. If the Member State that received the original notification fails to comply with the suggestions of the other Member States regarding further information or amendments in the testing program, it must give its reasons. If the Member States still cannot reach agreement or if any one of them believes, on the basis of detailed reasons, that additional information or amendments to the study programs are really necessary to protect health or the environment, the Commission may be asked to make a decision within the framework of its Technical Adaptation Committee. Thus, there is provision for verification and cross-checking at the Community level, although the system is likely to be slow and cumbersome, since official communication between national administrations is involved.

The EC Commission might ultimately decide to propose to the Council actions on a particular substance that would go further than the classification, packaging, and labeling provisions of 79/831/EEC. In this case, the Commission might decide to prepare a special directive; or it might decide to use an already existing instrument such as the Council Directive[9] under which polychlorinated biphenyls (PCBs) and vinyl chloride are regulated.

The United States

TSCA requires EPA to inform the public of its actions on chemicals for which it has received notification. The Act also provides a fairly complex mechanism by which EPA can, by rule, limit or prohibit manufacture of a substance or any other commercial activity involving it. The premanufacturing notification period can be extended by EPA to a total of 180 days. Notice of extensions and the reasons for them must be published in the *Federal Register*. Each month, the Administrator must publish a list of substances currently under examination, as well as a list of substances for which the notification period has expired since the previous month.

If the EPA Administrator decides to take no action to prohibit or restrict the manufacture of a chemical substance for which premanufacturing notification is given, he must publish in the *Federal Register* the reasons for not acting before the end of the notification period. However, publication of the reasons is not a prerequisite for starting the manufacture of the chemical.

The Administrator may issue a proposed order (to take effect at the expiration of the notification period) to prohibit or limit manufacture or any other commercial activity for the substance. He may do so if, during the premanufacturing notification period, he finds that he has insufficient information upon which to base an evaluation of the chemical substance and either (1) that it may present an unreasonable risk of injury to health or the environment or (2) that the chemical may be manufactured in sufficient quantity to enter the environment in substantial quantities or cause substantial or significant human exposure. The proposed order must be issued at least 45 days before the expiration of the notification period, and written notice must be given to the manufacturer. The manufacturer has 30 days after receipt of the notice from EPA to file objections. If the manufacturer does file objections, and if EPA wishes to pursue the matter, it is resolved in the courts. Alternatively, the manufacturer may decide to withdraw the notification.

If the EPA Administrator has enough information on which to base a determination that a chemical substance is likely to result in an unreasonable risk of serious or widespread injury, he may issue a proposed rule effective immediately upon its publication in the *Federal Register*. In order to do so, he must also determine that immediate action is necessary to protect the public.

In TSCA there is a direct connection between the notification of a new substance, risk assessment, and consideration of a wide range of potential controls. Notification creates the essential link between government and industry, setting in motion the entire system and creating a factual basis for the relationship.

THE ROLE OF THE EUROPEAN COMMUNITY AND INTERNATIONAL ORGANIZATIONS

International organizations now have no direct role in notification. This may not always continue to be the case, especially if countries move toward mutual agreement on goals of mandatory notification, consistent assessment of hazard, and exchange between countries of hazard assessments.

Such actions in the longer run may even lead to international agreements on mutually acceptable approaches for controlling existing chemicals, concerted international action on specific chemicals, more extensive sharing of information, and mutual agreement on guidelines for hazard assessment and risk analysis. All of these subjects are contemplated for future attention by OECD in an approach in which each step is influenced by what has already been done. Ultimately, this might lead to harmonization in which there will be "chemical passports" for trade in industrial chemicals.[10] As discussed in Chapter III, OECD expert groups have developed test guidelines (test protocols), a "base set" of tests, and good laboratory practices, and are dealing with step-sequence testing and confidentiality. Agreement in these key areas will help make notification systems of different countries more compatible.

Experience in establishing the U.S. inventory shows that substantial resources are required to develop a major register. At the international level, differences of terminology can render the establishment of such a register difficult. One of the OECD groups is currently working to establish a glossary of terms relating to chemicals.

The role of EC institutions in the notification procedure was apparently discussed at some length in the legislative process leading to adoption of 79/831/EEC. The proposal submitted to the Council of the Community in September 1976[11] provided a much more active role for the Commission, which would have been able to demand certain types of information from the Member States. This approach was rejected, but the Commission retains the responsibility for preparing the EC inventory and may also have access to information to supplement the summaries it receives. In view of the character of the Community, this may represent the most extensive role presently possible for an international body.

Chapter V

Risk Assessment and Control

Hazard assessment is the determination of the nature and likelihood of adverse effects as a function of dose or environmental concentration of chemicals. Risk is present when there is hazard and exposure to it. Thus, risk assessment combines the results of a hazard assessment with an estimate of the magnitude and likelihood of exposure to hazard.

Exposure is conventionally estimated in terms of the amount and/or concentration of a chemical in an organism's environment—for example, in the air or water in the immediate surroundings. Thus, "exposure," as the concept is usually used, could be taken to imply that the uptake of a chemical depends only on the amount or concentration of the chemical in the surrounding media. This is not necessarily the case, as will be discussed later. Nonetheless, it should be kept in mind that an assessment of risk, due to exposure to hazard, requires knowledge or an estimate of the uptake of a chemical.

Control measures influence and are influenced by risk assessment. Chemical risks may be controlled by a wide variety of measures such as limiting the production of a chemical, limiting the nature of its use, or placing the chemical in vessels or other containers engineered to minimize (or prevent) release to the outside environment. Such control measures can influence the "exposure to hazard" component of a risk assessment. Conversely, the estimation of risk may lead to the conclusion that certain control measures must be imposed.

The manner in which risk assessment influences control measures is mediated by judgment. Some risks are thought to be acceptable (reasonable), others unacceptable (unreasonable) and in need of control. The relative acceptability or reasonableness of a risk is generally not measurable in objective terms. It depends on a value judgment, taking the risks and benefits of the chemical as well as costs of control into account. If risks, benefits, and costs accrue to different people, there may be differing viewpoints on the equity and merits of different control actions. Since each of the parties can reasonably be expected to have a self-interest in the outcome, decisions regarding the acceptability or reasonableness of risk are increasingly viewed as societal in nature, to be made by a publicly accountable decision maker.

Any of a wide range of control measures may be applied to a chemical, ranging from labeling, which discloses hazard, through varying degrees of control of exposure, to use of an outright ban on commercialization. Each option may present a different balance of risks and benefits for manufacturers, workers, consumers, and others. Thus, each option may require its own risk assessment and its own evaluation for acceptability. Some of the principal choices are:

- to control;

- not to control;

- to decide that more information is needed before a decision should be made;

- to sensitize private decision makers to public concerns;

- to distribute information on risk so that risk choices can be made knowingly.

THE DECISION-MAKING PROCESS UNDER DIRECTIVE 79/831/EEC AND THE U.S. TOXIC SUBSTANCES CONTROL ACT

Notification provisions under 79/831/EEC have four principal functions:

- First, they describe the information that must be developed before a substance can be placed on the market, leading also to the creation of a body of information that may be used from time to time for reference and control purposes;

- Second, they permit classification of substances as dangerous;

- Third, they require labeling to warn of hazards for substances classified as dangerous, and packaging that meets prescribed requirements;

- Fourth, they require that substances be permitted by Member States to be placed on the market if notification, classification, packaging, and labeling requirements are met (subject to prescribed saving clauses).

Directive 79/831/EEC is addressed to Member States, not to marketers or importers of products, and must be implemented prior to September 18, 1981, in national laws that conform with the provisions of the Directive. As noted, the Directive constrains Member States from imposing control actions that would hamper placing a substance on the market if notification, classification, packaging, or labeling provisions have been met. The Directive qualified this prohibition in the following way:

> When a Member State has detailed evidence that a substance, although satisfying the requirements of this Directive, constitutes a hazard for man or the environment by reason of its classification, packaging, or labelling, it may provisionally prohibit the sale of that substance or subject it to special conditions in its territory.

Thus, the EC Directive does not prohibit controls to prevent "placing on the market" if there is "detailed evidence" of the type noted above, or if the grounds for the prohibition relate to a consideration other than "notification, classification, packaging, or labeling."

The U.S. Toxic Substances Control Act may be used to require notification to EPA, development of test data, disclosure to EPA of information, and labeling as well as other control measures. Although these functions of the Act are stated separately, they can in fact overlap—that is, they may be used jointly or separately at various stages of a substance's commercial life cycle.

New chemical notifications under the TSCA may lead to control actions by EPA, if the contents of the notice and other information available to EPA meet the following test:

> . . . there is a reasonable basis to conclude that the manufacture, processing, distribution in commerce, use or disposal of a chemical substance . . . or that any combination of such activities, presents or will present an unreasonable risk of injury to health or the environment before a rule promulgated under Section 6 can protect against such risk . . .

TSCA also permits controls to be exercised after the new chemical notification period ends. In other words, fully commercialized substances can be controlled, if a finding is made (under Section 6) that meets the following test:

> . . . there is a reasonable basis to conclude that the manufacture, processing, distribution in commerce, use or disposal of a chemical substance . . . or that any combination of such activities, presents or will present an unreasonable risk of injury to health or the environment . . .

Comparison of the language in these two citations shows that the test to be used for controlling substances is precisely the same, whether the substance is new or already commercialized. Thus, the control feature of TSCA can be viewed as occurring at any time, before or after commercial manufacture, with neither a greater or lesser test to be met upon expiration of the premanufacturing notification period.

The economic effects may, however, become more severe if control is not imposed early—since market positions will have been established, investments made, and jobs are then at stake.

The national laws implementing 79/831/EEC may also contain control provisions. One can assume that most countries will, indeed, adopt procedures to deal with control issues. Existing French and Danish law bear this out.[1]

EXPOSURE AND DOSAGE ASSESSMENT

Exposure to hazard is seldom easy to assess with precision because of the almost infinite number of circumstances under which commercialization of a chemical may lead to uptake of the chemical by humans or other species. The key considerations in assessing exposure to hazard are (a) the amounts (and concentrations) of the chemical in the media that comprise the environment surrounding an organism (as well as the history of the chemical's presence) and (b) the absorption of the chemical from these media by the organism.

To illustrate, the amount of a chemical in the air breathed by workers in a chemical manufacturing plant will be known in some instances, and assumptions can be made about the rate at which each individual actually absorbs the chemical through his or her lungs. Estimates of the rate of absorption of airborne concentrations may be easier to make for gases than for dusts, since, for example, some dust particles are too large to be breathed into the lungs.

The situation is frequently even less predictable for airborne chemicals used under less easily standardized and controlled conditions than those of the workplace, such as in the home. For example, exposure by inhalation of solvents from a paint will depend on the degree of ventilation and the size of the room being painted.

The relationship between skin contact and absorption through the skin is frequently not known. One may speculate, for example, that dusts of water-soluble chemicals might be more readily absorbed by people who are prone to sweat, and by people who tend to be careless about touching dusty surfaces. Again, the likelihood of accurate prediction decreases when consumer exposure is considered.

Some chemicals are used in personal-care products such as cosmetics, clothing, facial tissues, shoes, and soaps. There is deliberate skin contact with such products; in some instances—cosmetics, soaps—that contact is equivalent to deliberate contact with the chemicals in the products.

For many products, skin contact depends on migration of the chemical. This can be illustrated by widely divergent examples, such as migration of plasticizers from vinyl upholstery fabric, extraction of components of inks from books and papers, extraction of chemicals of varying types from leather, and extraction of residual catalysts, monomers, and additives from plastics.

Exposure by ingestion of chemicals is seldom, if ever, deliberate for workers in manufacturing plants; nonetheless, swallowing of inhaled dusts and volatile chemicals may occur. The consumer ingests some chemicals in products intended to be ingested, such as food and drugs. Other products not intended for ingestion may be swallowed—for example, drain-cleaning liquids, topical disinfectants, oven cleaners, and paints—particularly by children; intoxicating substances like methanol, though widely known to be harmful, are sometimes deliberately ingested by adults.

The kinetics of exposure are also important, since in most cases exposure will not be uniform over time. The intensity, duration, and frequency of each exposure need to be considered. Often, time-weighted average exposures are calculated; this is particularly true in occupational settings, where it is important to estimate the average exposure of workers to chemicals over the course of a normal working day. The actual amount of a chemical in a person's body will depend on complex relationships among rates of uptake, metabolism to other chemicals, and rates of excretion. Studies of such matters, known as pharmacokinetics, are necessary to understand the risks actually presented by the complex patterns of exposure encountered in actual occupational and consumer settings. The industrial hygienist and the industrial physician must deal with such considerations in a practical way even in the absence of perfect knowledge.

Although the study of toxic effects can be considered a science still in its early development, it is in many ways at a more sophisticated level of development than assessment of exposure and uptake. Even when people are exposed to chemicals by direct and relatively straightforward pathways, there are many difficult questions: How is exposure to be measured if it varies from time to time? Is eight hours of dosing with low levels of a substance more or less "exposure" than ten minutes of dosing with high levels of a substance? The science of assessing exposure to hazard is still relatively undeveloped in relation to what is needed for purposes of risk assessment.

Assessment of exposure to new chemicals may require agreement on a lexicon of uses for chemicals that in some manner suggests the degree of exposure expected to be encountered in each use. At present, there is no good way, for purposes of exposure assessment, to classify the many kinds of uses for chemicals, though some progress has been made in developing a nomenclature based on a chemical's function and the particular application in which this function is performed.[2] Potential for exposure is undoubtedly linked in a complex way both to specific uses and to the physicochemical properties of products and their component chemicals.

Without attempting to be comprehensive, it is important nonetheless to note that human and environmental exposure can occur through complex routes after the chemical is dispersed into the environment. While in the natural environment, the chemical may bioconcentrate in the food chain, or be chemically transformed into substances that are more toxic or less. Mathematical models of environmental distribution have been developed, but a complete environmental analysis of such processes is not a simple task. Precisely because the fate of a chemical in the environment is so difficult to predict, massive phenomena can occur before there is awareness of risk. Many of the more disturbing impacts of chemicals on man and on animals in recent years have been due to a substantial, yet unrecognized build-up of chemicals in the environment.

For human exposure, it is easy to conclude that exposure of many people to large doses of a chemical is of greater concern than exposure of a few people to small doses. In many cases, however, the exposures of greatest concern are less clear-cut: a few people (usually workers) are exposed to larger and more frequent doses and many people (usually consumers) are exposed to smaller quantities.

We need much more knowledge than we have about assessing exposure to hazard. The complexity of the subject assures that obtaining this knowledge will not be an easy task. In considering approaches toward simplifying the job, it should be noted that there is not at present even general agreement on the factors that must be taken into account. A lexicon of factors or sets of factors would be helpful so that all relevant exposure pathways are considered.

RISK ASSESSMENT—FACTORS TO CONSIDER

Risk can be visualized as deriving from two interacting factors: exposure and adverse effects. To construct scales of increasing effects and increasing exposure is not a simple task, since each depends on a variety of factors. A scale describing the potential for exposure might be based on a hierarchy of the following sort:[3]

- chemicals used only as intermediates (intended to be consumed by chemical reaction) in a closed reaction vessel;

- chemicals used only in such closed systems as electric capacitors;

- chemicals used in open systems, such as solvents in paints;

- chemicals used in close or continuing contact with or proximity to people, such as in household products and clothing;

- chemicals dispersed in the environment in large quantities, such as fertilizers.

Exposure can be expressed in terms of extensiveness, intensity, and duration, that is, how large a population is exposed to how much of the chemical for how long. The nature of the target organism (for example, humans, fish, animals, vegetation) and the likelihood of uptake by each kind of organism are also of obvious importance.

Surrogates may need to be used in risk assessment when information on actual exposure and effects is unavailable or incomplete. Frequently used surrogates include annual production data, uses of the chemical, and chemicophysical properties of the substance (volatility, solubility, distribution coefficients, and so on), but still other data or combinations may also be used. Human health effects are usually estimated from tests using animals. Data on environmental effects, if available at all, are usually limited to acute toxicity tests for a few animal and plant species, and surrogate information on the chemical's fate in the environment. Neither direct data nor surrogates are usually available regarding chemical interactions (synergisms or antagonisms between a particular chemical and other chemicals); hence, these are usually ignored.

The importance of setting priorities for risk assessment and communicating this to the public cannot be overemphasized. Frequently, the substances judged to present the highest potential for risk—on the basis of, for example, the kind of scale mentioned above—are not assessed first, for a variety of reasons:

- New chemical notification procedures establish a queue: new substances are considered in the order of their notification dates.

- Risk must be assessed on the basis of information: priority may be given to a substance simply because information is available for risk assessment; if information on a substance is very skimpy, it may be necessary to delay risk assessment itself until adequate information is developed.

- Public attention may be diverted to other substances by reports in newspapers, magazines, radio, and TV of specific chemical problems. Lacking any clear communication of priorities and the reasons for them by policymakers, the public and the media will look at each report in isolation from other problems. Political pressure may then develop for immediate action by the regulatory agency, since the substances on which attention is focused will usually be perceived to present a substantial risk.

In the absence of a well-conceived list of priorities for risk assessment and for allocation of resources, a regulatory agency may have no recourse but to give its attention to an *ad hoc* pursuit of each chemical currently in the focus of public attention. In fact, one could argue that this is the route by which chemicals have usually been selected for priority assessment.

RISKS, COSTS, AND BENEFITS

Under TSCA, EPA is required to consider the following factors before prohibiting or regulating commerce in, or particular uses of, a chemical substance or mixture:

- Effects on health and the magnitude of the exposure of human beings;
- Effects on the environment and the magnitude of exposure of the environment;
- Benefits for various uses and availability of substitutes for such uses;
- Reasonably ascertainable economic consequences after consideration of the effects on the national economy, small business, technological innovation, the environment, and public health.

One may look at the risks and benefits of a chemical, but it is simpler to compare different control options if the same information is expressed in terms of the costs and benefits of the regulatory options. For example, the benefit of a chemical in a particular use would be included in the cost of a regulation to prohibit the use.

Systematic assessment of benefits deriving from a particular chemical has advanced unevenly. The economic impact of producing a substance can sometimes be assessed in great detail in accordance with generally accepted procedures of market economics. Most producers undertake an assessment of these benefits to the firm before production begins, and, in the case of large-scale production, methods exist to analyze direct economic impact, including employment effects. The social benefits deriving from use of a substance can also be important. For example, some therapeutic drugs can be life saving; some involve the acceptance of very significant risks in return for even more important potential benefits. Where uses of a substance are less directly linked to an absolute societal or individual good, such as human life, but to important but relative ones (such as freedom or the pursuit of happiness), the assessment of social benefit becomes increasingly difficult.

The availability of substitutes is a relevant consideration in assessing benefits and risks. The consequences of substitution are difficult to establish, since comparable information is needed on all of the substances under consideration. In principle, it is desirable that all evaluations of risks and benefits be based on net effects, that is, for the substance in comparison with substitutes.

The continued use of chlorofluorocarbons, in the face of scientific evidence that these substances may produce substantial changes in the upper atmosphere, illustrates all of these difficulties. A few countries have decided to ban nonessential aerosol propellant uses; other countries are considering similar steps. No control action has yet been taken by any nation for nonaerosol uses.

The actions of chlorofluorocarbons on aerosol uses are proceeding with full recognition that there are substitute propellants and that these substitutes present risks of their own. (The speed with which substitution is forced can itself be a significant determinant of economic impact.) As to nonaerosol uses, carbons are the materials of choice as blowing agents in insulating foams, but there are other kinds of insulation that may be used in some instances. For most kinds of refrigerant uses of chlorofluorocarbons, however, there are no satisfactory substitutes.

Some uses of chlorofluorocarbons are probably more essential then others. For example, if refrigeration were to be made less readily available, public health hazards would develop in societies now extensively dependent on refrigeration of perishable foods. The use of air conditioning for private automobiles is more discretionary. Further, it is possible to explore ways in which chloroflurorcarbon losses to the atmosphere from air-conditioning units can be reduced.

Thus, the nature of the use, the availability of substitutes, the social benefits of the use, the economic consequences, and the assessment of the probability and magnitude of risk all enter into the chlorofluorocarbon equation.[4]

BALANCING RISKS AND BENEFITS

Balancing risks and benefits is an extremely complex process. Among the issues are who should participate in the decision and what factors should be included.

The Boundary between Reasonable and Unreasonable Risk

The determination of what constitutes an unreasonable risk is a societal judgment and is thus not amenable to objective analysis. While people may make judgments about what risks are unreasonable, and individuals are surely entitled to advocate adoption of their views, chemical control laws give governmer.t this authority. In the United States, TSCA assigns final decisions about unreasonable risk to the EPA Administrator, and not to any private individual or organization. Since all control measures imply some limitations of freedom of action imposed on some member of society, controls must be applied in conformity with constitutional procedures and other checks on arbitrariness. Each country has its own system of protection for fundamental individual liberties, and governmental control of hazards arising from chemicals must take these fully into account.

No definition of unreasonable risk that applies to all chemicals is likely to be very useful. For example, an unreasonable risk could be defined as one that, if continued, would produce more costs to society than benefits. Such a definition, however, would simply shift the question of unreasonableness to a debate over how costs and benefits are to be measured and weighed.

Interactions between Government and the Regulated Industry

At least for the near future, there will likely be continuing debate on the relationship between government and the regulated industry in deciding the acceptability of risk. It can be argued that none of the present toxic substance control laws relieves corporations of responsibility for the safety of the products they produce or of liability in the event of injury. There is no transfer of responsibility to government of the corporation's need to assess and control risk. The Directive 79/831/EEC does not presume that governments will necessarily conduct risk assessments of the chemicals for which notifications are received. On the other hand, it does not prohibit them from doing so, and there is some opinion that such assessments will be made. Similarly, in TSCA, the Act creates the opportunity for EPA to assess and control the risks that may be presented by a new chemical; but the Act does not require EPA to do so, and EPA is unlikely to undertake a careful risk assessment for every new chemical notice it receives.

Neither do TSCA or the EC Directive relieve companies of the obligation to pay for the testing and evaluation of their products. Under TSCA an elaborate mechanism is created by which the cost of testing may be apportioned among companies if testing is conducted because EPA requires it. Under 79/831/EEC, each company is responsible for its own testing costs, although companies may attempt to buy the right to refer to the data in another company's file by negotiation with the company that owns the file; there is no required sharing of costs. (France invites companies to share the costs of testing required by the government on an existing chemical.[5])

It is, however, with respect to the setting of standards for testing and control that governments intervene most directly under the new laws. Before the new laws were enacted, decisions on testing and control of chemicals in most segments of the chemical industry were made solely by business management groups. TSCA gives EPA authority to require testing, and to enforce control measures; therefore, business managers in the United States have lost their freedom to act solely on the basis of their own decisions. Government-imposed standards may exceed the standards, in extensiveness and quality, that a corporation would have established on its own; yet, in some instances, the reverse may be the case.

It is only if a corporation can accurately gauge EPA's standards for control, and decides to behave in a manner equivalent to these standards, that it can be sure the government will not override its internal decisions. Loss of sole control by corporations of these kinds of decisions, it could be argued, may have contributed to the level of concern by U.S. industry about TSCA and its implementation by EPA. There is, of course, a rational basis for this concern, since the decision-making process will inevitably be slower than before, and EPA may arrive at conclusions with which business managers would disagree. The situation also lends itself to controversy insofar as a measure of independence is taken away from business-management groups by the new law, and business leaders may still seek their former control over standard setting and decision processes so central to the commercialization of new products.

Here again, long-established social traditions apply that differ from one country to the next and are difficult to change, even for reasons of international harmonization. In many European countries, close relations have long existed between industry and government. In France, for example, a practice exists whereby an entire branch of industry enters into a voluntary agreement with the government to undertake certain measures for environmental protection over a period of time that may or may not be mandated by law. In return, the industry receives government aid both in partially financing the program and in obtaining the necessary permissions for planned investments.[6]

In many countries in Europe, industry has long been accustomed to sharing vital production information with certain government agencies and has come to accept that these data will be kept confidential as a matter of course. In the United Kingdom, major industries (not including the chemical industry itself) are nationalized, but industry information is still kept confidential, as if nationalization had not occurred.

The Public's Role

In view of the unspecific character of many toxic substances laws and the potentially controversial nature of policies for their implementation, public participation is viewed by many as a precondition for democratic policy decisions. The public is composed of many segments: industry, consumer and environmental groups, scientific and health professions, workers, and others. Because toxic substances laws are aimed at reducing risks, participation of representatives of those most immediately at risk may contribute significantly to proper decisions.

Countries have widely differing attitudes toward public participation in these matters, ranging from overtly supportive to candidly skeptical. Again, basic traditions play a vital role in determining what ultimately may or may not occur.

Public participation in policy formation within the framework of toxic substances laws may be effected at several stages in the process:

- The government or bodies responsible for decision making may organize hearings or invite general public comments and/or comments from professional groups, about general or specific proposals for chemical control, before and during decision making.

- Representatives of public interest groups, relevant professional groups, and those at risk may assist in the development of policies by participation in advisory committees.

- Decisions of governmental bodies may be open to judicial review by means of lawsuits from individuals or groups.

Although national traditions set the basic pattern of public participation within a nation, a number of unexplored issues exist with respect to international action. In countries with well-established traditions of public participation—such as the United States or, in the European context, The Netherlands—environmental groups are increasingly faced with a fundamental characteristic of international action: the primary actors in negotiations are representatives of the Executive. Parliaments are given an opportunity to say yes or no, but do not themselves normally have any say in the conduct of negotiation. As more issues need to be handled internationally, an effective erosion of parliamentary control occurs. Something similar is happening with respect to public participation. Where formal rights or traditions of public participation do exist, they can effectively be eroded by transfer of decision making to a less open or accessible international level, unless specific measures are taken to counterbalance this transfer.

The Process of Decision Making

The language of TSCA makes it quite clear that EPA must consider trade-offs among conflicting values in making determinations of unreasonable risk. The general criteria for determining key trade-offs are stated in TSCA as follows:

Authority over chemical substances and mixtures should be exercised in such a manner as not to impede unduly or create unnecessary economic barriers to technological innovation while fulfilling the primary purpose of this Act to assure that such innovation and commerce in such chemical substances and mixtures do not present an unreasonable risk of injury to health or the environment.

The selection of the control option that eliminates unreasonable risk in the least burdensome manner may be made in a qualitative, intuitive manner. There are advantages, however, if costs and benefits are quantified wherever possible.

Uses and Limits of Quantification. Quantification is not an end in itself, but is rather a means to make the reasoning behind a regulatory decision clear and explicit. However, there are at least two possible disadvantages to quantification. First, the amount of conflict and controversy over a proposal or decision may be increased if the basis for the decision is clearly revealed. Second, quantification may cause the decision maker to slight those elements that are not presented in quantitative terms, such as aesthetic value, effects on innovation, or the political impact of a decision.

On the other hand, although explicitness may increase controversy, it will also give greater focus and relevance to the debate, reducing the amount of uninformed or unconstructive rhetoric. In the past, controversy over decisions the bases of which were not articulated may have been muted because people assumed that the decision maker knew what he or she was doing. This is unlikely to be the case today. Rival constituencies are well organized to scrutinize important decisions.

It may be that some unquantified values will be slighted if the analysis is quantified to the maximum extent possible. However, because the final decision cannot be arrived at through mathematics, but only through the judgment of a decision maker who brings his/her own values and biases to the decision, unquantified values are just as likely to receive excessive attention as to be slighted. Also, it is not clear that the unquantified values lie more on one side of the cost-benefit calculation than another. The suffering attendant on a human death is unquantified, but so is the impact that regulation may have on technological innovation.

It would be of immense help to the decision maker if the different components of a decision could be made commensurable so that they could be aggregated and compared in some systematic way. Such an approach would allow the decision maker to compare the current decision to past ones. It would also provide people inside and outside government with a better understanding of the basis for the final decision. The traditional way for make disparate units commensurate, and then aggregating them, is by translating nonmonetary elements into money values. However, for some of the most important elements in health and safety regulations, such as lives lost and adverse health effects, it has not been possible to obtain monetary equivalents that command any general agreement. No single measure exists, in monetary terms, for such elements and the selection of a monetary equivalent is itself a decision heavily laden with value judgments.

For other reasons also, monetary values may not be good units to use in measuring costs and benefits. Their use often lends a spurious impression of certainty to the analysis. Perhaps most important, the use of monetary values strikes many people as callous and immoral. The notion of trading human lives against money is ethically repulsive to many people. This attitude undoubtedly helps explain why government agencies have been reluctant to do cost-benefit analyses.

In the past, the process of making trade-offs in health and safety decisions has usually been equated to comparing monetary values. But there is no logically necessary connection between the two. An alternative approach is to start with a tabulation of *all* factors to be considered, and then to identify those most relevant to each particular decision. Some of the fundamental issues are: How many different kinds of noncommensurate factors need to be considered (lives, money, personal health, aesthetic values, and so on)? How can the different elements be incorporated in analysis? How should future benefits and costs be compared with present benefits and costs?[7]

In the health and safety context, such questions have tended to obscure the fundamental need for some method, however basic, of systematizing and making explicit the trade-offs that every decision maker must make. Perhaps it is time to set aside attempts to find monetary equivalents and to focus on the need for explicitness as a realistic starting point in constructing a method of analysis more appropriate to regulatory requirements today.

Distribution over Time and among Groups.   Chemical production and use may affect future generations. For instance, the half-life of chlorofluorocarbons is such that, if consumption were to be stopped today, there might still be a significant negative impact on the ozonosphere for several decades; or, to cite another example, the effects of exposure to mutagenic chemicals may last into the distant future of our descendants. Several approaches may be taken when considering questions of distributive justice between generations:

- Some philosophies tend to prefer discounting procedures by which future benefits, costs, and risks are transformed into lesser present benefits, costs, and risks. At this extreme, the future may be heavily discounted.

- At the other extreme, it has been suggested that costs and risks should be internalized within one generation. Such a principle forbids carry-over of costs or risks into the next generation. It would prohibit the production of hazardous chemicals for which significant environmental residues are to be expected after the passing of one human generation.[8]

- Between these extremes, there are various possible principles that take serious account of future generations. One such intermediate principle is to judge the impact of current decisions on future generations, and to accept those risks to future generations that would be acceptable risks today.[9]

Distribution of risk among groups also needs to be considered. A decision maker in principle needs to know all of the groups that may be placed at risk by the proposed or actual commercialization of a chemical. Some affected groups are easy to identify, and will usually be taken into account; occupationally exposed groups fall into this class. Other groups such as the direct users of products are also easy to identify in some instances, though not always. The uses of a chemical may not be known to its manufacturer. For example, a manufacturer may sell a chemical to a distributor who in turn sells it to a compounder and then perhaps to a manufacturer of a finished product. Knowledge of use may be in the hands of one person, knowledge of risk in the hands of another.

Still other groups may be exposed to a chemical without having had any measure of consent or any awareness of the presence of risk. Children typically fall into this class for many types of products, as do adults in their exposure to chemicals from unsuspected sources such as residues on foods and chemicals extracted from pipes that carry drinking water.

These complexities suggest that decision makers are unlikely to know all the different ways people may be exposed to a chemical once it enters general commerce. In the face of such incomplete information, the conservative working hypothesis in risk assessment is to assume that a wide variety of people will be exposed to a chemical once it enters commerce, unless explicit and proved measures have been taken to limit the potential for exposure.

Voluntary vs. Involuntary Exposure. Not every person exposed to a particular substance knows that he or she is exposed; often, persons who are exposed do not know about the nature of the risk they are taking.

Clearly, this raises important issues: civil liberties in the United States or, in the European context, human rights.

In general, there is a greater openness of the decision-making process in the United States than in Europe, where more attention is given to communicating the results of a decision to the public. The greater willingness of nations in Europe to make administrative decisions in forums that are closed to the public, often secret, and the relatively greater freedom of European officials from challenges of their decisions in court would suggest a greater willingness in society to delegate decisions to authoritative figures, but not necessarily a lesser emphasis on informed consent and voluntariness of exposure.

Both TSCA and 79/831/EEC contain provisions by which labeling of substances may be required, to warn of danger. The relatively greater detail with which labeling rules are described in 79/831/EEC may in time be matched by EPA regulations under TSCA, and, in fact, labeling regulations are being drafted by EPA. An emphasis on labeling can be viewed as a commitment to an informed voluntariness in exposure to risk.

Catastrophic and Uncontrollable Events. Another controversial item is the yardstick by which health risk will be measured. Those involved in the development and implementation of health policies tend to view health risks in terms of the number of lives expected to be lost. There is suggestive evidence that several aspects of health risks do not surface in such estimates yet contribute significantly to the general public's perception and evaluation of health risk. For example, the belief that effects are controllable (which is not necessarily the same as actual controllability) tends to diminish perceived risk.[10] One large catastrophe tends to be taken much more seriously than a number of small accidents, adding up to the same number of victims. Carcinogenesis and embryotoxicity seem to be more dreaded than arteriosclerotic effects.[11] Voluntarily assumed risk is more acceptable than involuntary or uninformed exposure to risk.[12] These distinctions are only beginning to be understood, and it is difficult to predict how attitudes may evolve as the issues come into better focus and are the subject of wider debate.

Working with Uncertain or Incomplete Information. Hazard information varies in its degree of certainty. Well-documented, acute human reactions to chemicals stand at one extreme. For example, concentrated sulfuric acid always causes a reaction on human skin, and the effect is readily seen in laboratory animal tests; it is not a statistical phenomenon occuring in only a fraction of the population.

For certain chronic effects, cancer as an example, not every exposed individual will experience an adverse reaction; thus, not every individual person or laboratory animal exposed to asbestos will develop cancer. Yet society is beginning to accept the idea that chemical exposure can cause the effect, even though the relationship, for each individual, is statistical rather than certain.

The use of laboratory tests as surrogates for human experience has already been discussed at length, and it has been pointed out that some of the least expensive and least time-consuming tests for chronic effects bear only a probabilistic relationship to human experience. Sometimes a result is falsely positive, that is, the test is positive but in fact the substance does not cause an effect in humans. Sometimes a result is falsely negative, that is, the test is negative but in fact the substance does cause an effect in humans. Yet if the correlation is better than pure chance, the test result cannot be dismissed as having no predictive meaning. This kind of uncertainty plagues many, indeed most, laboratory animal studies, though to varying degrees; it is also a factor in the use of laboratory data to assess the fate of a chemical in the natural environment.

There is universal agreement that it is unacceptable to permit use of human exposure as the first testing ground for chemical substances when there are laboratory procedures with some degree of predictive power that can be used instead. The problem, and it is not an easy one, is to understand the consequences of using surrogate laboratory tests when one must deal with false positives and false negatives. It is costly to stop development of a new chemical because of a positive laboratory test that later turns out to be false; it is costly to proceed with development of a chemical because a laboratory test is negative and later learn that the substance does in fact cause human disease or disability. How one may balance these costs is discussed elsewhere in this chapter, but here it is necessary to introduce another option, namely, to refuse to decide until more certain information is available. This option is particularly important for new, untested chemicals when there is the opportunity to reduce uncertainty by obtaining some first bits of laboratory data. It is in this sense that a base set of information on new chemicals is particularly important.

But the decision maker cannot perpetually seek more information. There is no point at which surrogate information will with certainty predict the effects of a chemical in humans. The decision to commercialize is always made in the face of some degree of uncertainty about health and environmental risks, even if the best available laboratory testing has been done. It is increasingly important that decision makers and the public learn to accept the consequences of this inescapable need to make decisions on the basis of uncertain and incomplete information. All new developments involve some degree of risk; the actual risk may be greater or less than that which is perceived. The public process for making such decisions is at an early stage of development. The art of describing the reality of the decision-making process in credible, understandable terms is equally rudimentary.

CONTROL OPTIONS

Following is a relatively comprehensive listing of control options. It is taken from TSCA, and is presented here to display a range of options, not to provide a basis for comparison of laws. Control options may differ from one nation to the next, but it is reasonable to expect that each nation will want to exercise control of chemical risks so that unacceptable risks can be eliminated at least cost to society. This implies the availability of a wide range of options so that the most appropriate one can always be selected for use.

One or more of the following control options may be applied, by rule, under TSCA to the extent necessary to protect against unreasonable risk:

- A requirement (A) prohibiting the manufacturing, processing, or distribution in commerce of a substance or mixture, or (B) limiting the amount of a substance or mixture which may be manufactured, processed, or distributed in commerce.

- A requirement (A) prohibiting the manufacture, processing, or distribution in commerce of a substance or mixture for (i) a particular use or (ii) a particular use in a concentration in excess of a level specified by the Administrator in the rule imposing the requirement, or (B) limiting the amount of a substance or mixture which may be manufactured, processed, or distributed in commerce for (i) a particular use or (ii) a particular use in concentration in excess of a level specified by the Administrator in the rule imposing the requirement.

- A requirement that a substance or mixture of any article containing a substance or mixture be marked with or accompanied by clear and adequate warnings and instructions with respect to its use, distribution in commerce, or disposal, or with respect to any combination of such activities. The form and content of such warnings and instructions shall be prescribed by the Administrator.

- A requirement that manufacturers and processors of a substance or mixture make and retain records of the processes used to manufacture or process the substance or mixture and monitor or conduct tests that are reasonable and necessary to assure compliance with the requirements of any applicable rule.

- A requirement prohibiting or otherwise regulating any manner or method of commercial use of a substance or mixture.

- A requirement prohibiting or otherwise regulating any manner or method of disposal of a substance or mixture, or of any article containing the substance or mixture, by its manufacturer or processor or by any other person who uses or disposes of it for commercial purposes.

- A requirement directing manufacturers or processors of a substance or mixture (A) to give notice of unreasonable risk of injury to distributors in commerce of the substance or mixture and, to the extent reasonably ascertainable, to other persons in possession of such substance or mixture or exposed to such substance or mixture, (B) to give public notice of the risk of injury, and (C) to replace or repurchase the substance or mixture as elected by the person to which the requirement is directed.

- Any requirement (or combination of requirements) imposed may be limited in application to specified geographic areas.

At the final stage, when control options are weighed and chosen, there will likely be social and political factors that are unique or peculiar to each nation, since analyses and control decisions are influenced by social, legal, and political considerations as well as benefits and costs. There is great need for international cooperation to find approved methods of risk assessment, but application of the methods, for the time being, will likely occur on a national level.

INTERNATIONAL ACCEPTABILITY OF RISK

Nations have differed and will likely continue to differ in the extent to which they will accept risk to the health of their citizens and to the environment. Since such choices are value laden, they are reached by value judgments in each nation. Nonetheless, at the extremes of risk, there are conditions in which a consensus may exist. There may be chemicals for which most or all would agree that broad commercial use is unacceptable and limited use is appropriate only under the most carefully labeled and controlled circumstances. Similarly, at the other extreme, there may be circumstances where risk can be presumed to be so low that full commercialization is acceptable to all.

There may be pressures through GATT and other channels to minimize international differences in control of chemicals entering international trade. Harmonization among nations will depend in part on the extent to which dialogue among nations leads to commonly accepted views on the course of action that is most sensible, taking environmental, health, and economic considerations into account.

One way to view the problem is to emphasize international agreement regarding the information and analyses on which decisions will be based. With common data elements and a common format for their presentation, the opportunities for misunderstandings should be reduced, and the clarity of discussion should improve.

It must also be recognized that some risks deriving from chemicals are inherently international in character, either because of the way in which the chemicals are dispersed in the environment or because damage occurs outside national jurisdictions—for example, on the high seas or in the outer atmosphere. For such risks, national assessments will be incomplete unless they bring risks incurred internationally into focus along with the more usual evaluation of domestic risks and benefits. Attention to international risks may be generated by initiatives taken by one or a few nations, such as control of chlorofluorocarbons in aerosol uses, but ultimately effective control depends on nations addressing such issues in concert with one another.

Chapter VI

International Trade

International trade in chemicals and chemical products is already large and is growing rapidly. Total world chemical exports were estimated at over $122.5 billion in 1979.[1] Chemicals account for 11 percent of the exports of OECD countries and over 8 percent of their imports.[2] Large as it is, trade in chemicals is dwarfed by the volume of international trade in products that contain chemical substances. At the limit, this could be defined as encompassing virtually all manufactured and semimanufactured products entering international trade, as well as certain primary products that are treated with chemicals.

Differences in chemical notification, testing, and control policies have the potential to affect trade in many ways. As with all environmental, product-safety, health, and occupational safety and health measures, differences exist among countries in the pace, severity, and character of toxics regulation. In general, countries in the forefront of policymaking to protect the environment risk possible adverse competitive shifts in trade—certain exports may become less competitive in world markets, while certain imports may become more competitive in the domestic market.

Requirements for testing and notification of new chemicals are different from traditional environmental protection requirements in that they are not directly linked to the production process itself, but rather represent a cost that is like a product development cost. While the trade impact of environmental controls imposed on production processes has been studied[3]—the results are generally inconclusive—very little is known about the actual impact of technical requirements such as those created by TSCA and 79/831/EEC.

INTERNATIONAL TRADE AGREEMENTS
AND TRADE PRACTICES

The environmental community and the trade community know relatively little about each other, and there is thus far no mechanism that provides for assessing the relative merits of environmental and trade considerations at the international level, if and when there is a conflict. Nations engaged in international trade must find ways somehow to balance trade and environmental protection commitments.

The most important of the international trade agreements relevant to environmental protection in general and to toxic substances control in particular is the General Agreement on Tariffs and Trade (GATT).[4] Other rules exist at the regional level, as in the EC, where the Treaty of Rome commits member countries to the principles of internal free trade within the Community. Conceivably, UNCTAD, (the United Nations Conference on Trade and Development) could also prove an important factor as the position on toxic substances control in nonproducing countries comes more clearly into focus.

The GATT was originally envisaged as an integral part of an international trade organization to be established under the terms of the 1948 Havana Charter. The intent was to create a coherent set of rules for international trade, investment, and monetary relations in the postwar world. The Havana Charter was never ratified, but GATT remained.

Among the signatories to the GATT are most of the important producers of chemicals in the market-economy countries. Mexico, a rapidly growing producer, is not yet a member, however. Most of the socialist countries of Eastern Europe and Asia and many developing countries have not sought membership, in part because of difficulties in bringing domestic trade practices into line with the GATT articles.

The GATT, staffed by a secretariat in Geneva, essentially consists of a set of rules and procedures. These in turn serve as an umbrella for trade negotiations among individual countries. The main substance of GATT is contained in the Articles of Agreement, whereby countries undertake to apply negotiated tariff rates to imports of each other's products, to avoid discriminatory trade practices and the like. Trade negotiations, such as the 1963-67 "Kennedy Round" and the 1974-79 "Tokyo Round," are held under GATT auspices, and agreements reached are binding on the contracting parties after ratification.

The Tokyo multilateral trade negotiations resulted in the Agreement on Technical Barriers to Trade, called the Standards Code.[5] It is based on the principle that product standards should not be used to screen out imports through differential impact or administrative procedures. The Code goes a long way toward achieving the principle for both industrial and agricultural products. It accepts that industrial standards should not result in unnecessary obstacles to trade, and that imports should be treated no differently from domestically produced goods. Signatories of the Code will provide foreign suppliers with assistance in their efforts to comply with technical standards.

The Code itself does not set out technical standards or testing and certification systems, but it does establish a legally binding set of rules governing these, including oversight, complaints, dispute settlement, and redress procedures. Moreover, national standards are to be aligned with international standards where possible, and regional, state, and local regulations are to be brought into compliance with the Code on a best-efforts basis.

The preamble to the Code states that ". . . developing countries may encounter special difficulties in the formulation and application of technical regulations and standards" and proposes to assist them in their endeavors in this regard. Such assistance will also be extended by private, subnational, regional, and international standards organizations, as appropriate, to assist corresponding bodies in developing countries in fulfilling their obligations under the certification schemes of importing countries. Signatories of the Code will also make special efforts to notify developing countries of technical standards on products of special export interest to them. A Committee will oversee the application of the Standards Code.

The United Nations Conference on Trade Development (UNCTAD) serves as the principal forum for the discussion of North-South trade and other economic issues. Its membership is far larger than that of the GATT, encompassing essentially all UN member countries. The focus has been to provide the developing countries with easier access to the markets of the developed countries through reductions in tariffs and nontariff trade barriers, to stabilize the markets for developing-country exports, and to increase financial flows to the developing countries. UNCTAD has achieved partial tariff liberalization and some liberalization of nontariff barriers. In the latter area, the traditional UNCTAD view has been that developing-country suppliers are disproportionately affected because of their more limited ability to comply with health and safety standards, customs formalities, and other requirements that are frequently considered nontariff barriers.

Governments are, by these international agreements, limited in the manner in which they impose health and environmental controls that might also be viewed as trade barriers. On the export side, governments are constrained in their use of subsidies to help domestic industry cope with cost increases attributable to toxic substances control. There are few constraints, however, if a government wishes to create restrictions to prevent export of substances banned at home. On the import side, international agreements relate mainly to licensing, government subsidization of premarket testing and related costs, and industrial standards affecting internationally traded products. In all three of these highly technical areas, there are well-established and evolving rules of international behavior that constitute significant constraints on toxic substances policy.

Clearly, any differential impact that is more adverse on imports than on domestically produced goods would have a potentially protective effect, quite apart from any abuse of toxic substances control for intentionally protectionist reasons. Beyond these issues, there are problems of labeling and the highly sensitive question of confidentiality versus disclosure of product data and testing information, both discussed in greater detail in Chapter VII.

RESPONSIBILITY FOR INTERNATIONAL TRADE NEGOTIATIONS

In the United States, responsibility for negotiating international trade matters such as those arising under the GATT has been shared by the Departments of Commerce, State, Treasury, and Agriculture. Such agencies as the Federal Trade Commission, Food and Drug Administration, and Environmental Protection Agency have been involved when issues concerned their mandates. In a recent reorganization of the U.S. trade bureaucracy, principal authority on trade matters has been focused on the U.S. Trade Representative and the Department of Commerce, thus reducing the nominal authority of the other agencies, though preserving the principle that they will be consulted on matters affecting their interests. Through liaison, backup support, and related activities, the U.S. Trade Representative will provide a single voice for the United States on trade matters, particularly in international trade negotiations, but is required to consult with a newly created Trade Policy Committee and with any affected regulatory agency.

In the Community, the main issue concerns the relationship of EC and national authorities in external negotiations. Through a recent decision of the European Court of Justice,[6] the principle has been affirmed that the EC has authority over all external negotiations relating to matters for which it has legislated internally. As a consequence, the EC is likely to play an increasingly important role in international negotiations, although certain matters remain unclear. Since EC and national legislation often overlap, and the relationship between the two is evolving steadily, it is not possible to define explicitly where one begins and the other ends. For example, in the area of chemicals control, the Community is responsible for those aspects covered by 79/831/EEC (such as notification) but in all others (such as application of control measures), national law will predominate at the outset. Thus, increasingly, both the Community and Member States have signed international conventions, declaring that each does so only for those aspects for which it is competent. In the context of the GATT, the Community, generally plays a very important role, because one of the foundations of the Community is the existence of a common customs tariff, and the authority of the Community to negotiate in this area is unchallenged. In the matter of the Standards Code, however, the more complex relations between the EC and the Member States apply.

Given the ambiguity of who represents the EC at international negotiations, having the Community negotiate does not necessarily lead to a simplification of proceedings. At major meetings, it is always the head of the national delegation from the country chairing all Council meetings at the time (a responsibility that shifts in alphabetical order every six months) who speaks for the Community.

TRADE IMPACTS OF TOXIC SUBSTANCES CONTROL LEGISLATION

Anytime some manufacturers are subject to more costly regulatory requirements than others, competition may be affected and nontariff barriers created. There are many such possibilities for barriers to trade as a consequence of toxic substances control laws, as exemplified by TSCA and 79/831/EEC. These are largely caused by the imposition of requirements to protect health and the environment. The rights and obligations of governments to develop and enforce such requirements are not subject to debate, nor is the mandate that all products sold in a national market must be in compliance with established standards. The key requirement, rather, is that technical standards should not be unnecessarily trade-restrictive in effect, and should not be used to discriminate against foreign suppliers. Differences in actual control measures may, of course, pose significant barriers. However, trade distortions may also emerge as a result of testing and notification requirements, as well as treatment of proprietary information.

There is no implication in this discussion that measures will be taken by nations for the purpose of deliberately creating trade distortions in their favor, though this is, of course, possible. Instead, the emphasis here is on examination of the unintended trade distortions that may arise as a consequence of serious attempts to follow health and environmental policies judged to be desirable on the basis of national criteria. By examining these potential trade distortions, ways may be found to eliminate or minimize them to the extent possible, while preserving national criteria for health and environmental protection.

The differences in the EC and the U.S. approaches to new chemical notification may cause problems that can affect access to markets. Foreign manufacturers first have to ascertain precisely what is required of them, and this may involve substantial search costs, delays, and uncertainties. Some substantive issue areas have been discussed at length in earlier chapters: how much information is required, the standards for development of the information, when it must be submitted, the extent of review, the handling of confidential information, and exemptions from notification.

Another area of potential importance involves subsidies and countervailing duties. It is at least conceivable that certain countries will choose to subsidize their manufacturers' testing costs and other expenses attributable to toxic substances policies. In deciding how to implement their respective policies, governments will have to pay attention to the possible trade-policy repercussions of subsidies that convey competitive advantages.

THE SPECIAL CASE OF MIXTURES AND ARTICLES

One of the more difficult problems in toxic substances control relates to the origin of substances. They may logically enter a nation's commerce only by one of the following routes: extraction from natural materials in the nation (products of mining, agriculture, and so on); manufacture within the nation (synthesis by a manufacturer); importation as a substance; importation as part of a mixture; importation as part of an article; and transport into a nation through the environment (air, water, and so on). For a nation to know the new substances entering its commerce, it must know about new substances entering through any of these routes. If one route is not covered, the logic of the control process is destroyed.

The American Importers Association has noted that there are 200,000 importers and customs brokers who bring items into the United States every year; some of these items are articles containing hundreds or thousands of chemical substances. For example, one automobile contains more than 15,000 separate components comprised of an unknown number of chemical substances.[7] Due to the complexity of the task, lack of information, and lack of technical resources, many importers cannot begin to distinguish whether the goods they import contain new chemical substances. Hence, the notification of the new chemicals in all imported articles, at the time of importation, is not considered to be practical.

Within a nation with a chemical control law, domestically produced articles will necessarily have been manufactured from substances and mixtures already subject to control. Any serious attempt to achieve comparable enforcement for chemicals in imported articles by requiring notification at national borders would likely be frustrated because of the complexity of the task. In the absence of such enforcement, domestic manufacturers of comparable products may be at a competitive disadvantage. In the

United States, it has been suggested that, to address problems of equity between domestic manufacturers and importers of articles, chemical substances produced by a company in quantities of less than 1,000 pounds per year and used solely within that company to produce an article should be exempt from new chemical notification requirements, though EPA should, it is suggested, be told of their existence.[8]

It is not clear whether the Directive 79/831/EEC excuses from notification substances used exclusively within a company to manufacture articles, if the substances are placed on the market only as components of articles. If such substances are in fact excused from notification under 79/831/EEC, then the exclusion would appear to apply at any production level, and Member States would not be informed of the existence of these chemicals.

Similar kinds of difficulties can also exist if an attempt is made to require notification for all components of imported mixtures. The issue is particularly troublesome with respect to the minor components of mixtures. It is likely that in some instances neither the importer nor the manufacturer of the imported product will know, or be able to learn, about some minor components.

Although the logic of toxic substances control requires knowledge of chemicals that enter a nation's commerce as components of imported articles or minor components of imported mixtures, there are questions about the practicality of dealing with all such substances by requiring notification in the importing nation at the time of importation. Alternatively, there could be notification of such substances in their countries of origin. This would be of little comfort to the nation importing the mixture or article, unless it had assurance that substances made for export were controlled by other nations to a mutually satisfactory degree—through, for example, international treaty.

THE CASE OF MULTINATIONAL COMPANIES

Multinational corporations play an important role in the chemical industry. How these firms respond to international differences in measures involving their internationally traded products may be of considerable significance.

A multinational company with many plants in many countries has the option of serving a particular market from several production points. In the absence of health/safety policy agreements among the major producing nations, and to the extent that corporations react to environmental or health/safety policy measures by shifting from a producing plant in one country to another plant in a different country, it would appear that the actions of multinational firms may actually increase the sensitivity of the international economy to differential national conditions, policies, and instruments. However, it is often not easy to shift production among plants, and it is costly and time consuming to build new plants.[9]

The vertically integrated multinational may have various sources of supply within the firm and may, in the face of environmental or health controls, shift from one source of intermediates and raw materials to another. Similarly, if environmental controls impair productive capacity at any one plant, it may be possible to shift to other plants without disrupting the firm's overall operations.

Nevertheless, it is important not to overstate the flexibility of multinational corporations in responding to toxic substances controls. Multinationals are not single corporate entities. Because no international corporation law exists, multinationals must incorporate in each country. While they may be controlled from one source, legally the subsidiaries in different countries must act as separate units, that is, establish separate accounting, billing, tax accounting, and so on. This means, for example, that a transfer of a substance from a company in Switzerland to its subsidiary in the United States is legally indistinguishable from a transfer to a completely independent U.S. company. Thus, though subsidiaries in different countries may have a common center for financial and policy control, they are subject to restrictions and general practices dictated by the laws and practices of the nations in which they are established.

In fact, there is a tendency within some multinational corporations to resolve these internal difficulties by producing to the most stringent standards encountered in the countries they are dealing with. Such an approach, which preserves economies of scale, also has distinct attraction to central management, which has a built-in inclination to limit diversity between production units so as to be able to maintain control. This approach is, of course, only possible in a situation where national approaches are sufficiently compatible so that the more stringent standards adopted by the corporation also meet all other requirements fully.

Chapter VII

Transfer of Information

Before governments can control a potentially hazardous chemical, they must obtain adequate information about its toxicity and how people are exposed to it. Therefore, a primary focus of laws like TSCA and 79/831/EEC has been on the generation, evaluation, and transfer of information about chemicals and their uses.

Earlier chapters on notification and hazard assessment have considered how information is generated and then transferred from industry to government. The chapter on risk assessment addressed some of the issues involved in combining hazard data with other types of information to make control decisions. This chapter discusses the issues that arise from the needs of governments, corporations, and the public for information about chemicals, and the frequently conflicting need of private interests to control access to that information.

Those who take part in the process of determining the degree to which risk from chemicals should be controlled by society must have sufficient information to perform their task. The public has an interest in knowing what steps the government is taking to control chemical dangers, and what the basis of these actions is. Members of the public need to be able to adjust their conduct to limit exposure to hazardous chemicals. Those who use or process chemicals must be able to devise safe procedures for use and disposal.

The types of information these people need and the forms in which it may be communicated vary considerably. Regulatory agencies need to know the health and environmental effects of chemicals at different levels of exposures, and the levels of exposure likely to occur. Chemical processors need, in particular, to know about reactivity and/or performance characteristics, purity, stability, and aspects of the chemical's safe use and disposal. Workers (including researchers, factory workers, and transporters) need to know the risks to which they may be exposed, how to handle the chemicals safely, and measures to take in case of accidents.

Within the limited space available on package labels, consumers must be informed how to use and dispose of chemicals safely, and how to deal with emergencies. Many kinds of organizations, including business, labor, public interest groups, and local governments need information about the basis of government chemical control decisions.

International organizations, governments, and the public need to be informed about the potential impact of and the possibilities for controlling chemicals that are traded internationally. Even if a nation does not have its own chemical production facilities, it will need sufficient information about chemical properties and effects so that it can assess risks and establish appropriate controls for imports.

Some chemicals and chemical wastes are transported across international boundaries by movement of air and water. Information about the effects of these substances on health and the environment also needs to be transferred internationally. In many instances, groups receiving information may take an active part in defining the information they need, in developing additional information, and in defining suitable measures for control of risk.

The available information about a chemical may not be adequate to meet all needs. In the first place, much of the information about the health and environmental effects of existing chemicals is, in varying degrees, unknown or uncertain. Further, because common international standards for laboratory practices and testing procedures are just beginning to be developed, scientists and regulators may not yet have confidence in information obtained from some laboratories, particularly those in other nations. Then, too, information generated by chemical manufacturers or processors may not be available, because it is closely held for reasons of commercial advantage.

A company has a financial investment in the tests it has performed and the products it has developed. It may want to consider part of the information about the chemical—such as its chemical identity or intended use—a trade secret. And it may feel that a degree of secrecy about testing information is necessary to prevent competitors from piggybacking on the research investment.

There is one tradition, perhaps more highly developed in the United States, that asserts the right of access by the public and concerned nongovernmental organizations to information sufficient for evaluation of chemical risks and review of government control decisions. The public in many countries participates through a variety of procedures with public officials in the development of governmental policy on technological issues.[1]

There is another tradition, more highly developed in Europe, that asserts the right to a relationship of confidentiality between business and government.[2] This tradition permits a high degree of information exchange between a company and government officials, but excludes the general public and nongovernmental organizations from access to the information supplied by industry to the government, and from involvement in ongoing government policy decisions.

Neither of these traditions excludes all aspects of the other. In all instances, there is recognition that some kinds of information under specified circumstances are legitimately trade secrets once disclosed to government by a firm; these trade secrets must be protected by the government against disclosure to the public. Also, there is general recognition by all that some kinds of information about health and environmental risks must be disclosed.

Thus all systems need to take into account the identification and protection of some kinds of information. The word *confidential* is widely used and almost universally understood. This should not, however, obscure the fact that it has no universal legal meaning: it may mean the practice of restricting access to certain persons, to certain institutions, or to groups of people, depending on the law, political tradition, or the circumstances of a particular situation. The extent to which the information contained in notifications is restricted in its further dissemination—and, therefore, not available to scientists, health professionals, industry, the public, other agencies of the same government, government contractors, other levels of governments, or authorities in other nations—is one of the major, unresolved issues of chemical regulation and another way of defining the subject of this chapter.

The question of information transfer must respond to the need for broad access to some information and controlled access to other (confidential) information. This may be described in terms of a tension between protection of industrial trade secrets and disclosure that is adequate not only to inform the public of risks to health and the environment, but to permit informed public participation in discussion of these health and environmental-quality issues.

European countries, which license chemical plant operations, rely on close cooperation between industry and government. For example, British industry voluntarily gives extensive information to the government with the understanding that it will not be disclosed further. The political balance in the United States lies closer to the public disclosure end of the scale, influenced by a strong environmental movement combined with a broadly based trend toward public access to government documents as a matter of right.

The clearest current illustration so far of these different political cultures is in the handling of health and safety studies. TSCA allows most such studies that EPA is likely to obtain, including data, to be made public; the EC requires only that an interpretation of test results be made public.

Individual nations, the EC, and international organizations are beginning to define possible solutions to problems of information collection, storage, and transfer by focusing on the development of data networks and labeling systems. These data and labeling sytems will need to be examined for international compatibility, and must in time become adequate to enable governments and users to evaluate risks associated with specific chemicals used in specific ways. For these reasons, and because of the complexity of the information that needs to be handled, the development of such systems will be very slow and expensive.

INFORMATION TRANSFER

Various national laws, and the European Community, have established frameworks governing the transfer of information to government by industry, within government, among governments, and to the public by government. Chapter IV described transfer of information from industry to government; this section will focus on transfers within government, among governments, and to other groups from government.

Within Government

In most countries, control of chemicals is divided among authorities for health and environment and may also involve such offices as transportation, labor, and industry. The proposed law for the Federal Republic of Germany provides that the dossier of information about a new chemical goes to the Federal Institute for Occupational Safety and Accident Research. However, four other agencies also must evaluate the information. The French law requires numerous agencies to take part in the Council that evaluates data. The U.S. law gives the Environmental Protection Agency the lead role in toxics control regulation as well as coordination of information dissemination, but six agencies have related regulatory authority and many more have research or advisory responsibilities.[3]

For a government to carry out its responsibilities effectively, information may need to be transferred among national agencies, to contractors working for these agencies, to administrative courts or hearing officers, and to other levels of government. Practices in transferring information among agencies now vary widely even within countries. These differing practices become an international issue when a nation in which information is not shared among agencies, or shared in limited ways, is reluctant to make information available to another country with more open practices.

Limiting the use of confidential information to the agency that collects it prevents the possibility of public disclosure by another agency with less strict procedures. It keeps information in the agency with authority to collect it. Some laws specifically forbid agencies to share confidential data for these reasons. In the United States, this is true for the Consumer Product Safety Commission, and the Food and Drug Administration. The Toxic Substances Strategy Committee, a group created by the President to co-ordinate overall government toxic substances control, noted in its report that, in fact, as the result of inconsistent laws and policies, there is little sharing of confidential information among agencies in the United States.[4]

While nontransference of confidential information is still a common practice among agencies, the high cost of information gathering and the wastefulness of duplicative development of toxicological data—in the face of shortages of facilities and trained professionals—indicate a need to find ways to share information.

Some U.S. laws, in recognition of the broad and interrelated natures of toxics issues, allow the transfer of confidential information among agencies charged with protecting health and environment. This transfer encourages joint agency action and eliminates the need for duplicate reporting. TSCA specifically allows such dissemination. The Inter-agency Toxic Substances Data Committee, established by TSCA, is working toward common policies and procedures to allow for more sharing of confidential information without sacrifice of security. The Committee is addressing issues such as who has access to the data, computer security, and penalties for unauthorized disclosure.[5]

Policies for interagency exchange of confidential information have already been suggested by another committee, the U.S. Interagency Regulatory Liaison Group, which consists of five agencies with mandates in chemical control. It has proposed standards for protecting confidential business information.[6] Industry has, quite naturally, shown a keen interest in interagency exchange of confidential information and has already gone to court to force agencies to develop strict procedures.[7]

The proposed chemicals law in the Federal Republic of Germany would provide for detailed regulations to govern cooperation among agencies taking part in evaluating the technical dossier submitted on a new chemical. The documents themselves are to be forwarded to the evaluating agencies and summaries to the Community.

Much of the information on effects and exposure needed by agencies involved in toxics control can be gathered and analyzed by private research organizations—that is, contractors who provide specialized skills when needed. This makes it unnecessary for government agencies themselves to develop capabilities used only sporadically. It could, of course, be argued that any assessment requiring the use of confidential information should be performed within government agencies. However, as the range of issues in notification, testing, exposure assessment, and control has broadened, contractors have played an increasing role. While earlier U.S. laws did not address the release of confidential data to contractors, such release is permitted under TSCA (and under the law dealing with pesticides).[8] EPA regulations now require notice to a company if confidential data are being disclosed to a contractor. These regulations also address conflicts of interest and impose penalties on the contractor for unauthorized release of information.[9]

Many countries make provisions for release of confidential information in legal proceedings, but there is now little consistency in the way the release is handled. Among the practices are the following:

- *Release of the information only to those directly involved.* This has the advantage of limiting the release of information to few people, but presumably makes it available to all who need it. It is not clear whether public interest groups would necessarily be considered directly involved, however. The Directive 79/831/EEC uses this approach.

- *Selective release.* Because of particular expertise some groups might be able to contribute to a proceeding if they had access to the necessary information. Agencies might be given discretion in releasing information to people they think are qualified provided there are sanctions against intentional disclosure of the information by such people. In the United States, the Toxic Substances Strategy Committee has suggested this approach.[10] A similar pattern has also been proposed by the Deutsche Forschungsgemeinschaft, the German national science foundation.[11]

- *Summaries.* Summaries of information may be enough to provide adequate information for some purposes. If at a suitable level of generality, their use assures that no confidential data will intentionally or inadvertently be released. Some U.S. agencies follow this practice.

In federal systems, state or provincial governments as well as local governments have a responsibility for health and environmental protection. Which information collected at the national level these other levels should have access to is a matter of considerable debate. If confidential data were available to state or provincial governments, the chances of its being released would be greatly increased, some argue, since state or provincial governments may not have strict control procedures. TSCA does not provide for the release of confidential data to the states. In the Community, this would need to be regulated by national law. TSCA does, however, allow release if there is imminent danger or if necessary to protect health and the environment. In emergency situations, the proposed German law provides for a state-federal action plan, but the law makes no mention of transfer of confidential information.

State and local governments are continually facing situations where information about toxic chemicals is required. Collecting this information is expensive and may put an added burden on industry. Thus, ways need to be explored to permit access by state and local governments to information collected at the federal level. Development of security procedures as stringent as those at the federal level might be one alternative. Another alternative might be for state and local agencies to designate a limited number of individuals who personally may inspect confidential data at a central federal location and then use this information in their own organizations (but not disclose it to unauthorized persons).

Another point at which confidentiality issues may arise is the transfer of information between executive agencies and legislatures. Under TSCA, committees of Congress have the right to obtain confidential information from EPA, and may use this information in their oversight of the law. In Europe, parliaments do not exercise such close oversight over administrative actions, except where hearings on a specific occurrence of major importance take place—normally requiring a vote on the floor of the assembly to be instituted. Only then does the question arise of transfer of confidential information to parliament. In the case of the Italian parliament's hearings on Seveso, substantial amounts of confidential information were ultimately communicated.[12] On the other hand, the German parliament's committee on nuclear safety was unable to obtain a copy of an important contract, known to be in the government's possession, covering processing of nuclear wastes—even after major portions had been published in the press.[13]

Among Governments

The difficulties of communicating within a government are multiplied among governments; there are additional barriers of language and culture as well as the sensitivities of national sovereignty and concern about trade barriers. Regional and international organizations and national laws all play a part in transfer of information among nations.

European Community. The EC's Directive 79/831/EEC is an enforceable agreement among nations on the exchange of information for chemical risk assessment. Under the Directive, the technical dossiers for new chemicals that are marketed or imported will be transferred in summary form, or in full, to the Commission and EC Member States. Each Member State may have access to the complete data, subject to the condition that nations need not provide the data to other nations where there are less strict measures for protecting confidential information. The Community is also addressing the need for data networks and test standards. An Environmental Chemicals Documentation and Information Network (ECDIN) is being established to give national agencies access to resources of the European Community.[14]

Organisation for Economic Cooperation and Development. The Organisation for Economic Cooperation and Development (OECD) plays a leading role as an advisory organization on both policy and technical matters involving control of chemicals. OECD is particularly suited to do this because of its membership, which includes all the countries that are actively in the process of implementing toxic substances legislation. However, OECD will likely need to broaden the scope of agreements on particular issues to include nonmember countries.

OECD has been given the task of developing proposals for internationally concerted action in a variety of fields: agreement on test methods; a code for good laboratory practice; treatment of confidential data; a glossary of key terms; methodologies for economic studies; expanded information exchange; and so forth. The OECD confidentiality group is examining the extent to which members might share chemical information. The group is first identifying the types of data involved and then the mechanisms used in different countries to provide access to and, at the same time, protect information about chemicals.

A procedure to exchange regulatory information established in 1977 by OECD is now used by nineteen countries and six international organizations. It has thus far been used mainly to report administrative actions by the United States, Canada, and Sweden. It has also been used to request information.

United Nations. The United Nations Environment Programme is developing an International Register of Potentially Toxic Chemicals (IRPTC); the Register will eventually include both scientific and regulatory data. Also, a number of other programs collect data on special categories of chemicals or effects. The World Health Organization (WHO) and the Food and Agriculture Organization (FAO), for example, operate a Food Standards Program which develops standards to protect consumers and avoid unfair trade practices for food additives and pesticide residues. WHO also has an extensive program on the evaluation of the effects of chemicals on health. (See Chapter II.)

Export of Hazardous Substances.   Nations with chemical control laws generally apply these laws less strictly to exports than to imports and domestic products. This may put the countries without control laws— particularly the primarily importing countries—at a disadvantage. While each country can be expected to want to make its own decisions on the risks and benefits of a substance, importing countries often do not have the information on which to base decisions, or the technical and policy expertise to evaluate available information.

The disparity between the information likely to be available to producer and importer nations is generally recognized. Efforts are being made at international and national levels to develop improved policies on the export of hazardous substances. The major issues involved are: how best to transfer information to importing countries, and how to define the circumstances under which exporting nations might limit exports of hazardous substances or delay export until authorities in importing countries have had adequate time to examine information.

Policies are required on the types of information to transfer, to whom, and in what form. Notifications, of shipments, hazard data, and regulatory information need to be summarized in a manner widely understood, since both scientific and regulatory terms can be obscure. Because industry's need to protect trade secrets may make it difficult to provide some types of information, such as detailed uses and exact volumes, a means of protecting confidential information must be worked out.

TSCA requires EPA to notify countries to which a substance is exported of the availability of testing data and regulatory actions taken under the law. But experience with notification under pesticide regulations indicates that this type of communication is difficult to carry out effectively. An executive order is being drafted to improve and standardize U.S. approaches to export of hazardous substances.

The OECD Chemicals Group is considering the information needs of government administrators and users of chemicals in importing countries.[15] Additional efforts are probably necessary to ensure that the information is provided in a useful form. The conditions under which an exporting country should take the initiative and limit or ban exports of hazardous substances also must be explored.

The Public and Nongovernment Organizations

Information transfer to the public may be viewed as satisfying a number of purposes: to give the public the information it needs in order to take part in and to review societal decisions; to enable individuals to make their own decisions about the use of chemicals; to fulfill the obligation of government to keep the public informed; to satisfy the individual's right of access to the information.

It is in the transfer of information between the government and the public that nations differ most significantly in their administrative practices. In most European countries, extensive efforts are often made to involve long-established groups in consultative processes. The assumption is that everybody who has an urgent need to know and to participate will be brought into the process by official action. In the United States, there is a much greater tendency to leave the initiative to any person interested. The emphasis, therefore, is on making information publicly available. (See discussion below on "Public Access to Information vs. Proprietary Rights.")

Nongovernment participation in activities at the international level generally has been limited to industry groups. In OECD, for example, the Business and Industry Advisory Committee provides a route for industry participation on expert committees. The Trade Union Advisory Committee has not been as active. U.S. public interest groups are working with EPA to arrange membership on OECD expert committees.

INFORMATION SYSTEMS

Information systems dealing with toxic substances control may take decades to build. They must serve the diverse needs of manufacturers, regulators, users of chemicals, researchers, labor groups, public interest groups, workers, health professionals, educators, journalists, and many others. The obstacles are formidable: the large scale of the enterprise, the complex and rapidly changing nature of the information base, the lack of standardized formats and terms, the need to provide broad access while protecting confidential data, and so forth.

Information Networks

In the United States, the Interagency Toxic Substances Data Committee is charged with designing and coordinating a system to collect and disseminate to other agencies data submitted to EPA under TSCA. A report, required by the Act, has outlined the needs such a system should meet.[16] It recommends a chemical substances information network to link over 200 existing systems with one another and with new information systems developed under the Act. The network is now being developed under the aegis of the committee.

In Europe, the Environmental Chemicals Documentation and Information Network (ECDIN) is now in a pilot phase. The program is carried out partly by the Ispra Establishment of the Commission of the European Community's Joint Research Centre in northern Italy, and partly through contract research in universities and at other institutions. Its goal is to provide reliable information on environmentally significant chemical products. ECDIN will handle information in the following data categories: chemical nomenclature and other identifiers; chemical structure information; physical and chemical properties; chemical analysis data and methods; supply, production, and trade; transport, packaging, handling, storage, and hazards; use and disposal; dispersion and transformation of the chemical in the environment; effects of the chemical on man and the environment; regulatory data; and occupational health data.[17]

For nations that primarily import chemicals, the United Nations Environment Programme's information system—the International Register of Potentially Toxic Chemicals (IRPTC)—may become particularly important.

Formats are different for each data system, which makes linkages among them difficult. Standardization of terms is a particular problem. Information on chemicals is now stored in many different ways: by trade names, common names, generic names, or chemical structure. When information is requested about a particular chemical, one cannot be sure that one is actually getting all the information about a chemical, because of the different names under which information may be stored. This problem can be overcome by assigning numbers to specific chemical structures. The Chemical Abstract Service (CAS) number can serve this purpose and is widely used. In connection with the TSCA Inventory, a start has been made toward assigning numbers to the significant minority of commercial chemical substances that have variable or unknown composition. There is no standard system for numbering mixtures.

Different types of users have different needs from data systems. A scientist may need raw scientific data, while a journalist may prefer an interpretation of the results of testing. In addition, confidential information needs to be protected; this may require two separate systems, one for public use and one restricted to certain approved users. Confidential data might be aggregated to create nonconfidential summaries for the public file.

Many different viewpoints must be considered in designing internationally acceptable data networks. International conventions may ultimately be
necessary to deal with some of the issues.

Labels and Labeling

Labeling is the information link between the manufacturer of a chemical
and its user. For most chemicals, this link is the most direct means of
informing the health professional, consumer, transporter, processor,
commercial user, and factory worker about hazard. It therefore creates an
opportunity to limit risks. Labeling may describe the substance, its properties, hazards, safety advice, modes of treatment in the event of injury, and
other information. It can take many different forms: labels, documents,
programs that warn or instruct about the hazards of a chemical.

Existing chemical labeling systems, such as those used for transport and
in the workplace, have generally emphasized warnings, safety advice, and
treatment of acute effects. Changes are being made in labeling systems to
include consideration of a broader range of effects, particularly those due
to chronic exposure.

The 1967 EC Directive, 67/548/EEC, subsequently amended covers
classification, packaging, labeling of dangerous substances. It originally
provided for only four classes of dangerous substances: toxic, harmful,
corrosive, and irritant. An expanded scheme under 79/831/EEC (the sixth
amendment to 67/548/EEC) has fourteen classes: explosive, oxidizing,
extremely flammable, highly flammable, flammable, very toxic, toxic,
harmful, corrosive, irritant, dangerous to the environment, carcinogenic,
teratogenic, and mutagenic. Substances classified as dangerous must be
packaged and labeled in prescribed ways. Statements such as "not harmful" or similar phrases are not permitted.

Labeling is one of a number of controls authorized under TSCA. It is
generally considered the least burdensome and stands at the other end of
the scale from banning a substance. Classes of substances judged to be
dangerous are not explicitly stated in TSCA, but EPA may identify substances or categories of substances that, to prevent unreasonable risk, must be
marked or accompanied by warnings or instructions about use, distribution in commerce, and disposal. Also, a voluntary standard known as the
American National Standard for the Precautionary Labeling of Hazardous
Industrial Chemicals (ANSI)[18]—is widely used, and EPA is now developing
a regulation under TSCA that draws heavily on ANSI practices.

All of these systems, those of the 1967 and 1979 EC Directives, ANSI,
those under development by EPA, as well as a number of other labeling
systems now in force, call for the classification of chemicals according to

their hazards (dangers). Warnings and instructions on labels are then chosen to describe the nature of the hazard.

Classification into categories of hazard is based on the results of specific kinds of tests; for example, LD50 ranges are used to define acute hazard classifications, and hence the warning statements to be used. As already noted, the Directive 79/831/EEC describes several new classes of dangerous substances, including those substances that cause cancer, birth defects, and genetic effects. The U.S. law also does this. Appropriate tests for these effects are not yet specified in the EC Directive or in TSCA, however. Since test results are the basis for classification, it will be particularly important to develop compatible interpretations of test results to establish an internationally accepted classification system.

While there is fairly general agreement that known chronic effects need to be labeled in some way, there is much less agreement on how to handle uncertain or unknown effects. One way of dealing with untested substances is to label them as untested. The EC Directive recognizes this for substances exempted from full notification (such as those produced at less than one ton per year); until labeling is possible for these substances in full accordance with the Directive, labels are to bear the warning "Caution— substance not yet fully tested."

Relatively little attention has been devoted to evaluating how effectively labels communicate information about hazards. Warnings of chronic effects that may not occur for 20 to 30 years are more difficult to convey effectively than warnings about acute effects. Even more difficult is describing these chronic effects when the relevance of the test results to humans is likely, but uncertain, based on laboratory testing.

Labeling should provide enough information about risks so that people can understand the risks and how to avoid or minimize the likelihood of injury. Labeling can help processors make well-informed decisions on uses, and can be used by manufacturers and processors in establishing rules intended to prevent injury to workers.

Effective communication becomes even more difficult when a label must be understood outside the country in which a chemical is manufactured and the label is first affixed. Internationally compatible approaches to labeling need to be developed in five areas:

1. *Use of Symbols and Signal Words.* The U.S. voluntary system (ANSI) uses a skull and cross bones for very toxic chemicals. Otherwise, it relies on three levels of signal words—*Danger, Warning, Caution.* The EEC has symbols for six categories (an exploding bomb for explosive substances, a flame over a circle for oxidizing substances,

a flame for those that are extremely flammable or highly flammable, a skull and cross bones for toxic and very toxic substances, a St. Andrews cross for irritants, and a symbol showing the damaging effects of an acid for corrosive substances). Other symbols are being considered for the new categories of dangerous substances. A recent report on labeling[19] suggested that one new generic symbol be used to designate severe hazard, that a broad educational program be started to assure familiarity with this symbol, and that symbols of the type now used (skull and cross bones, and so on) be treated as a second-level warning about the specific danger.

Considerable agreement among nations has been reached on transport labels for hazardous substances and, in another area, on traffic signs, thus setting a pattern for eventual harmonization of symbols and standard phrases denoting chemical hazard.

2. *Language on Labels.* Many questions complicate the selection of language on labels of products intended for export. What if the final destination is unknown? What if a country has many languages? How will effective communication be established with the many people who are illiterate? One approach, already mentioned, could involve use of a generic, severe-hazard warning symbol widely understood to mean *"Wait. Do not use this product until someone reads the hazard warning label to you."*

The Directive 79/831/EEC permits an EC Member State to require the use of the country's official language(s) on labeling for dangerous substances placed on the market in that country.

3. *Color Codes.* The EC requires particular colors for symbols and for background on labels of dangerous chemical—black on an orange-yellow background. The Swiss have a color code that goes from black to red to yellow, depending on the degree of toxicity. There are no obvious reasons why a single approach, rather than many different ones, would not be preferable, though change in the face of long-standing use is not easy, as is now being seen in attempts to establish widespread use in the United States of a metric system of measurement.

4. *Risk Statements.* The EC uses 42 standard statements to warn users about the hazards of dangerous products—for example "Toxic if swallowed" and "Danger of cumulative effects." The manufacturer determines the most appropriate statement for substances, except that the choice has already been made and published for a group of about 800 substances classified under the Directive. The ANSI voluntary standard uses similar statements. Thus, for example, a

label for a substance highly toxic if inhaled reads "May be fatal if inhaled" and has the signal word "Danger" on it.

5. *Back-up Information.* It is often not possible to get as much information as needed on a label because of space limitations. Package inserts now accompany many pharmaceutical products. Material Safety Data Sheets (MSDS) are widely used by the chemical industry to provide more extensive information to employees in manufacturing plants, to commercial users, and to health professionals. The types of materials for which an MSDS may be prepared include raw materials, intermediates, and sometimes even wastes. Among the issues that need to be addressed are the essential contents of such backup material and how to handle uncertain data, or lack of data, particularly for chronic effects.

Past negotiations to harmonize labeling have focused particularly on transport, where such labeling is essential for safe handling and to prevent trade barriers. Labeling systems for rail, road, inland waterway, sea, and air transport systems are governed by different acts and regulations in most countries. Organizations such as the International Air Transport Association regulate labeling for international shipment. There is also a United Nations Labeling System.

Differences among nations on which hazards to label and how to do so can foster miscommunication, and could have adverse effects on trade. The United States, the Member States of the EC, and other interested nations may decide to develop a uniform standard to govern the labeling of hazardous chemical products. Such a standard could draw on the best features of present standards in these nations and in EC Directives. Differences of current practice would need to be resolved. The principal issues include: (1) the ways by which hazardous chemical products are classified, including ways by which mixtures may be classified based on the hazards of their component substances; (2) the methods used to communicate hazard warnings and other necessary information on container labels, including the use of symbols and standard language statements; (3) the types of information required on a container label; (4) the design and placement of labels on imported containers; and (5) procedures by which all nations may participate in the technical amendment, as necessary, of any aspect of a labeling system to which they all subscribe.

PUBLIC ACCESS TO INFORMATION
VS. PROPRIETARY RIGHTS

Directive 79/831/EEC and TSCA reflect the different overall approaches to information control that have evolved in the EC and the United States. The

EC provides broad protection for information, but cites five types of information that are to be divulged: trade name, physicochemical information, ways of rendering the substances harmless, the interpretation of test results and who performed them, and precautions and emergency measures.

The attitude toward confidential information at the federal level of government in the United States has changed in the past 15 years. Before, an industry could make a broad claim of confidentiality, and the information would probably not be disclosed except perhaps in summary form or in a legal proceeding. The Freedom of Information Act (FOIA), passed in 1966, makes many government administrative documents available to the public with specified exceptions. It allows, but does not require, an agency to exempt trade secrets and commercial and financial information from release. In the past, many agencies have not had clear policies to handle exemptions under the Freedom of Information Act for information claimed to be confidential. There has been wide discretion for agencies to decide which portions of documents to release. As a result, industry has been unsure what will be protected, and nongovernmental organizations have found it difficult to get information.

New regulations issued by agencies such as EPA are clarifying this situation. EPA regulations[20] list the following as criteria to determine valid claims of confidentiality: confidentiality has been asserted when submitted; the company is protecting the information itself; no statute requires disclosure of the information; and disclosure will harm a competitive position. The regulations require that the company be notified if the information is to be released by EPA. The regulations also allow redress. Still, there is probably greater access to administrative documents from the U.S. national government than is common in other countries or in some states. For example, Virginia specifically exempts confidential information gathered under its toxics law from release under its state freedom of information act.[21]

Information given to EPA under TSCA that is exempt from disclosure under the Freedom of Information Act may not be disclosed by EPA except under certain limited circumstances (if necessary to protect health or the environment against unreasonable risk, for example) or to certain persons (such as congressional committees). TSCA specifically allows the release of health and safety data for substances distributed in commerce or for which notification or testing is required, except that two types of data are protected: data that would disclose processes used in manufacturing and data that would disclose the proportions of chemical substances in a mixture.

France has had legislation along the lines of a freedom of information act since 1978.[22] It is too soon to know how it will be interpreted; given France's administrative traditions, however, it seems unlikely that detailed data on health and environmental effects will be made public.

National differences of attitude toward confidentiality are rooted in traditions of industry and administration and government, and in historical modes of industry/government relationships. In countries where industry is unhappy about the prospects of the disclosure of information, administrators are often equally unhappy. That is, the confidentiality issue appears, perhaps more than any other issue, to be deeply rooted in national tradition and legal codes of wide scope. This increases the difficulty of harmonizing differing national approaches.

For example, the United Kingdom in general has had a history of preserving confidentiality and protecting industrial data submitted to government authorities. One of the benefits of this practice has been that the government has tended to have a lot more data given to it voluntarily by industry, without having to exert pressure to obtain it. Another factor is the reason for transferring the data in the first place. In the United Kingdom, under laws governing worker health and safety, the obligation is very firmly laid on the manufacturer to transfer to his work force data about the health, safety, and uses of the substances, so that workers may take appropriate precautions under any circumstances in which they may be exposed to that substance. This provision does not imply or require the intervention of government in any way in the process. At the same time, the process occurs in a manner that gives government the ability to enforce some control if the necessary actions don't take place. The U.K. approach has worked for many years and has had very great benefits. It may prove completely inoperative in other countries, however, since it depends on the specific pattern of relationships that have developed in the United Kingdom over a very long time.

Under TSCA in the United States, the release of information to the public comes about not through an administrative decision on the part of EPA or because of the wishes of a few people, but is broadly based on the Freedom of Information Act, other statutes, and general public expectations. To expect a change specifically within the narrower context of TSCA would go against trends that are widely accepted in the United States. To deny information that has to do with public hazard is politically impossible.

Thus, this problem must be solved on a much broader basis than TSCA or 79/831/EEC. It involves protection of trade secrets, the right for people in the society to be informed about health and safety issues, and public participation in public decision making. Nevertheless, there may be a means of reconciling the need for public access and protection of proprietary data. Procedures could be devised to guarantee property rights to information even after public disclosure. Some kinds of intellectual property are, of course, already covered by patent law, which permits public disclosure and provides specific legal protection of proprietary rights.

Much of the attention in this book has focused on toxicity information where initial approaches to information control in the EC and the United States clearly differ. However, data on uses, production volume, and chemical identity also require compatible handling, since such information is needed to assess risk and can be even more sensitive than health and environmental toxicity studies.

For example, knowledge of chemical identity aids in evaluating test data and in assessing structure-activity similarities to other chemicals. But a manufacturer often considers chemical identity to be proprietary. Identity may, in itself be commercially valuable, or, for a chemical intermediate, it may give some indication of the process used to make another chemical.

The use of generic names has been suggested as a compromise between using exact names that disclose chemical structure and trade names that may give little or no hint of structure. Fully acceptable rules for stating generic names have not yet been developed. The generic name should give the scientist fairly specific information for hazard assessment, yet should be constructed to conceal the exact structure. Generic names can be used in a number of ways:

- *Use of a generic name for a specified period of time.* The need for confidentiality of identity is greatest in the first few years after a chemical is marketed. After that, competitors have had an opportunity to analyze the substance and perhaps determine its identity, and the company has also had an opportunity to establish its market position and to get some return on its investment. The Directive 79/831/EEC allows a new chemical to be listed in encoded form for three years unless it is classified as dangerous. The U.S. proposes to allow use of a generic name in health and safety studies until manufacture.

- *Generic name with no time limit.* When confidentiality is claimed, the U.S. inventory allows chemicals to appear with generic names. No time limit is given.

- *Generic names except for hazardous substances.* The actual identity of a chemical may be so important in cases when the chemical is dangerous that it may be in the interest of public health and environmental quality to make it available to the public. The Directive

79/831/EEC follows this principle. This gives the public access to identity only after the chemical is classified as dangerous.

- *No confidentiality for chemical identity.* Structure-activity relationships can suggest hazard, and many groups, particularly labor groups in the United States,[23] are asserting their need to know chemical identity so that they can properly and fully evaluate health risks.

Any of a number of approaches can be used to reconcile needs for public disclosure with claims that the information is confidential. Several of these approaches are described in the following paragraphs.

Summaries have often been used as a means of informing the public of test results. The EC Directive allows this practice and requires that interpretations of tests be made public along with the name of the organization performing the tests. Only government authorities are required to be given access to the dossier itself. During the first ten years after notification, any other company producing the substance must also perform the required tests or obtain permission from the first notifier for use of the data on file in the notification. This, in effect, gives each notifier exclusive rights to control the information it developed.

TSCA specifically allows health and safety data to be made public (except where such release discloses process information or proportions of a mixture). Test data developed under a TSCA testing rule must be published within 15 days of receipt and be available to any person. The U.S. law provides for sharing testing costs for substances subject to a rule for testing or listed on a so-called "risk list" of substances that present or may present an unreasonable risk. (No substance had been listed as of August 1980.) Thus, a manufacturer of a new substance is not reimbursed for information submitted with a new chemical notification unless one of these two conditions (tested under a rule, on the "risk list") applies, in which event others who produce or import the substance within five years (or the period it took to develop the data) would have to reimburse the first producer for a portion of the testing costs. However, U.S. experience with reimbursement under its pesticides law shows that such procedures may be cumbersome and may not reimburse companies for the true market value of data.

Another approach, differing from current EC and U.S. provisions, would be to allow companies "exclusive use" of their data for a period of time extending over several years and also to require that the data be made publicly available. The data could not be used as part of a notification by another company without the agreement in writing of the company that developed it. In effect, each company submitting data in a notification would need the permission of the originator of the data. Such exclusive use provisions can be useful in several circumstances. First, U.S. exclusive-use rights could be extended to EC notifications; this would prevent companies from using, in EC notifications, information released publicly in U.S. notifications. Second, should data in EC notifications be made public, a modification of this procedure (involving mutual exclusive use rights to data in the EC and the United States) could be used to protect a company's proprietary rights to data. Third, should TSCA be changed to conform with the EC requirement that each manufacturer and importer must submit a separate new chemical notification, adoption of exclusive-use provisions would protect proprietary rights to data in the EC and create proprietary rights to data in new chemical notifications in the United States.

Exclusive-use provisions of these kinds can help meet industry's concern that the value of data is not necessarily the cost of generating it but rather a function of the success of the product in the marketplace. At the same time, the public availability of health and environmental information would allow broad review of the chemical's risks and benefits.

Exclusive-use provisions, as described above, would offer protection for data relating to products marketed in EC Member States and in the United States, whether manufactured in these nations or imported. The process obviously would be even more valuable if the geographic area of agreement could be broadened to include still other nations or groups of nations, and might best be handled even initially on a broad international basis.

Chapter VIII

Policy Options: Harmonization and Implementation

The original concept of this book was to create a basis for informed discussion of transnational issues that affect a nation's choices of toxic substances control policies. The document was not intended as a polemic in favor of harmonization; nor is it now. Yet it was obvious even as this project was started that unnecessary national differences of approach are undesirable since they may seriously frustrate efforts to identify and control risks associated with production, use and disposal of chemicals, and may also disrupt patterns of international trade. Thus, harmonization is a positive goal that needs to be actively sought. This is the goal toward which OECD is directing most of its efforts, with noteworthy success. The greatest efforts in OECD and the greatest immediate opportunities are for international agreement on systems of new chemical notification, and the nature and quality of the information in such notifications.

From this perspective, it is particularly important that the issues set out in this book be made the subject of extensive and public international debate. This should provide a means of discovering internationally acceptable solutions and of assuring the necessary political will at the national level to put the needed measures into force.

Such a debate would be facilitated by a variety of measures, including the organization of meetings to inform and to build consensus—perhaps convened by national authorities—between the various groups who have an active interest in chemical control issues: government, industry, researchers, consumers, public interest groups, and the press.

A HIERARCHY OF ISSUES FOR HARMONIZATION

Harmonization of transnational policy suggests an active effort by countries to develop or reorder national policies to achieve internationally agreed upon goals. Thus, harmonization is something less than standardization—generally a variety of acceptable ways can be found to attain defined goals—but something more than coordination. In addition, harmonization may be applied to narrow specific policies or to broad policies and strategies.

Without wishing to minimize differences of approach, it is noteworthy that TSCA and 79/831/EEC share major common features. Each of these laws:

- establishes the concept of an inventory and the concept of a new chemical substance;
- establishes the concept of notification as appropriate for new chemical substances;
- requires industry to provide technical and commercial information to government authorities;
- deals with assessment of chemicals and the role of industry in this process;
- identifies the types of information that must be submitted or considered.

Similarities like these cannot be assumed to be fortuitous or self-evident, because there are approaches of fundamentally different kinds that could have been adopted. In fact, discussions among countries have taken place since the early 1970's and have resulted in marked similarities of approach and harmonization of broad strategies. Noteworthy formal international contributions can be found in recommendations of the UN[1] and the OECD.[2]

But what motivates this drive for international harmonization? A number of advantages can be listed:

- consistent world-wide protection of health and the environment;
- elimination of potential non-tariff barriers to trade;
- stabilization of the regulatory environment for the chemical industry (instead of needing to satisfy many different regulatory systems, chemical companies would face a consistent set of requirements in different nations);
- reductions in resource expenditures through efficient use of laboratories, toxicologists and other experts, and government officials.

In fact, none of the participants in the creation of chemical control policies can afford not to agree on principal issues, in the face of limited information, technical resources, materials, and time.

The opportunities for harmonization are greatest in those areas least constrained by differences of law, national self-interest, or outlook. For this reason, it is important to consider the context created by TSCA and 79/831/EEC, since the practical alternatives for harmonization are largely defined by these laws.

There is at the present time considerable momentum toward international harmonization. It is, important, however, that the nature of the process be understood. Harmonization of testing, notification, and control of chemicals is not a one-step, all or nothing affair. Any attempt to deal with all of these issues in one great step appears bound to fail. What is required is a fairly long series of steps, spread out over a number of years, to deal with the issues in an orderly sequence.

There exists a very real hierarchy of issues for harmonization, and this hierarchy needs to be respected. At any one time, several issues may be on the international agenda simultaneously, but at different stages of discussion. Certain issues should not be tackled too early if their solution is still beyond reach; attempting to deal with such issues too early risks bringing the entire process to a halt.

The first level of harmonization concerns agreement on language: definitions of the problem, as well as of more technical aspects, particularly definitions of terms such as "chemical substance" and "impurity" as well as nomenclature for specific commercial chemicals, including those that are not identifiable by a definite chemical structure. Common definitions of substances on U.S. and EC inventories, coupled with agreement within OECD on a glossary of terms are likely results of current efforts; one can expect that the problems arising at this first level will be surmounted. These issues are at an earlier stage of discussion within the more comprehensive framework of United Nations agencies.

The next level concerns testing procedures. Issues to be dealt with here include good laboratory practices and test protocols. The goal is clearly mutual acceptance of reliable test data. Once agreement is in sight on these matters, it is possible to deal in more detail with the definition of minimum test information requirements, that is, a base set of tests. Within OECD, the basic structure of agreement on these issues is visible.

Dealing with these testing issues would create the basic conditions for the next step: agreement on which tests to use and when they should be conducted during the course of assessing hazard. This leads fairly directly to decisions about step-sequence testing, now also under study in OECD.

At this stage at the latest, it becomes necessary to consider information about production volume, use, and other indications of potential exposure. This exposure information, not derived from testing, serves both as a means of determining the need for more extensive testing and as an element of a risk assessment.

This opens the way, next, to discussion of the format and the means of communicating the results of testing by industry to governments, that is, the conditions of notification. Differences between premanufacture (U.S.) and premarketing (EC) notification schemes must be dealt with insofar as they may have an impact at an international level, as must the roles of whatever list or inventories of notified chemical substances are created. The obligation of first and subsequent manufacturers, marketers, and importers must be clearly established.

Finally, international agreement can be sought on:

- the manner in which risk will be assessed;
- how acceptability of risk will be evaluated;
- the appropriate control measures that should be applied where risk is considered unacceptably large.

It is likely that practical resolution of these three issues will ultimately best be achieved by institutionalization of an open international dialogue. That would mean that all those concerned will be able to have a voice in these key phases of the process, will begin to better understand each other's interests, and will find avenues toward greatest mutual agreement.

SETTING PRIORITIES AMONG CHEMICALS

A key characteristic of the current situation with respect to control of chemicals is the lack of resources to deal simultaneously with all relevant issues. Testing facilities and trained toxicologists and ecotoxicologists are in short supply. So, too, are highly qualified national administrators, time on the agendas of international bodies requiring long-distance travel and multi-lingual discussion and, last but not least, the resources of non-governmental bodies of all kinds. Even when some of these resources can be expanded, financial constraints must be taken into account and priorities set insofar as the use of available funds is concerned.

To avoid a situation where debates about what to do next in the face of an overload of issues take up time that is needed for the discussion of substantive matters, it is important to keep in sight the ultimate goal—the protection of man and the environment from unreasonable risks arising from the production, use, and disposal of chemicals. Given the differences in political, administrative, social, and economic conditions between nations, it must be realized that the pathways leading to this universally accepted goal may be very different, though they must meet at the key points where harmonization is absolutely necessary.

All of these matters point to the need to select some issues for priority attention. The decision to focus at this time largely on new substances in the EC—simultaneously implying the need to define which substances are new—represents one such decision on priorities; the decision not to apply the base set to small volume products or to polymers in the EC is another.

A certain division of labor among nations is likely to prove useful, and emphasis on different issues by nations may ultimately prove constructive. For example, the European Community relatively single-mindedly pursued legislation on new substances, leaving aside a number of issues that were explicitly emphasized in the U.S. approach. The United States, which may ultimately benefit from some of the solutions on new chemical issues defined in the EC, has divided its attention more evenly between new and old substances, considering in particular certain aspects of dealing with existing chemicals, such as setting priorities for testing. These U.S. actions on old substances will ultimately be drawn into the international debate and contribute to maintaining its momentum.

ACCESS TO INFORMATION AND DECISION MAKING

A substantial part of the future debate about chemical control issues will concern the separate but overlapping needs of:

- multiple government agencies, private individuals, and groups who need access to information relevant to the identification and control of chemicals that can be injurious to human health or the environment, and

- manufacturers and other companies who need protection of proprietary rights to information they have developed or acquired.

Often, demands for information by agencies of governments, by foreign governments, trade unions, public interest groups, and individuals will be perceived by companies as an attempted infringement of the fundamental right and freedom of an owner of property, in this case intellectual property, to full control of that property.

Those outside the circle of trust can perceive such secrecy as depriving them of a fundamental right to full information on potential and real risks of injury to themselves, to the environment, and to future generations.

These two broad viewpoints are unlikely to be completely reconciled by even the most rational and extensive discussion. The differences are fundamental. Yet important accommodations between private freedoms and the needs of the community are traditionally recognized as necessary. Proponents of full control of proprietary information by the owner, and, on the other hand, full disclosure of information relevant to health and the environment will undoubtedly continue to struggle for acceptance of their respective points of view. The underlying issue is an important one and will need to be resolved in an acceptable manner sooner or later. The sharp divergence of opinions therefore sets the tone and context for a necessary public debate.

What is important from the point of view of developing practical and acceptable systems for control of chemicals is not to focus unduly on the question of access to information. That issue is so difficult that it unnecessarily carries the risk of sabotaging the entire process of harmonization. What is needed instead is a willingness to deal with this matter only when it needs to be faced, and only to the extent that it must be faced, within the context of the other issues on the table.

Thus, when dealing with the issues related to information contained in a notification, it is necessary to define both needs for protection of proprietary rights and needs for access in relation to each category of information. For example, where health and environmental test data are concerned, accommodations may be reached that would not be possible for the broader question of access to all kinds of information. One option, taken in TSCA, is to permit access to health and environmental data except in instances where certain kinds of proprietary information are involved. (In TSCA this occurs where the data would reveal the proportions of a mixture or the nature of the manufacturing processes.) Another option, presented in the preceding chapter, is to protect proprietary interests and simultaneously to provide full public access by introducing the concept of "exclusive" rights of the developer of information to use of that information, for a period of time. This concept has similarities to the concepts of patent or copyright protection. The more extensive disclosure of health and environmental data to the public in the United States than required elsewhere will eventually erode the proprietary value of a body of health and environmental data, unless some measure such as "exclusive" use is employed to protect property rights in the EC in the face of public disclosure in the United States. Member States of the EC have not yet dealt with this problem, though it is difficult to see how it can long be avoided, since many chemical products are marketed in both the EC and the United States.

When dealing with hazard assessment, it is necessary to acknowledge that chemical identity may itself provide meaningful clues regarding toxicological effects, persistence, bioaccumulation, and environmental distribution. The importance of chemical structure as an indicator of environmental distribution and toxicological effects will likely increase in the years ahead because of ongoing studies of structure activity relations (SAR). There are several ways in which conflicting points of view regarding public disclosure of chemical structure might be handled. For example, chemical names can be required to be disclosed after a specified period of time. Under 79/831/EEC a substance name may appear on a list in encoded form for a maximum of three years. Chemical names will then be revealed, presuming the list is made publicly available. A further step is the provision in 79/831/EEC that calls for public disclosure of chemical names for substances classified as dangerous. Still other accommodations may appear increasingly reasonable as SAR are perfected. For example, public disclosure of chemical identity could be required for chemicals in particular structural classes that are generally accepted as associated with adverse health or environmental effects, such as nitrosamines as a class.

Many other kinds of information have been claimed to have proprietary value. In particular, the publicly available copies of TSCA's new chemical notifications sometimes have many parts blanked out because the information is claimed to be confidential. Even the name of the company is sometimes withheld. In fact, some information that would have been disclosed in time if notified under 79/831/EEC may be withheld indefinitely under TSCA. The key point is that if the entire problem of access to information cannot practically be dealt with at any one time, at least part of the problem can be addressed in the context of issues in public focus at any given time—while other aspects of the problem can be deferred for later attention.

The same can be said of public access to the decision-making process. In the United States, such access is accepted as a matter of course in most aspects of government operation. The same degree of access cannot be claimed for most situations in Europe. There is no short-term prospect of dramatic change in this regard. However, experience during the 1970's, particularly in the area of land use and environmental law, demonstrates that incremental change leading to increased public access to governmental decision-making processes is possible. Indeed, the willingness of government officials to discuss toxic substances issues with environmental groups at a June 11-14, 1980, meeting in Bonn is a sign that the concerns of these groups in this regard are being heard.

INTERNATIONAL MOVEMENT OF CHEMICALS

Chemicals move internally by distribution through the environment and by trade. Distribution of chemicals through the environment across national boundaries, sometimes even on a global scale, can be highly complex and difficult to trace. The patterns of international trade are also exceedingly complex, since virtually all nations import chemicals and chemical products, while only some nations are substantial manufacturers and exporters. A substance that has been exported from a producing nation may be processed into products elsewhere, for example, and, in this new form, reenter international trade, perhaps even reenter the commerce of the producing nation. Complexities of these kinds are important, and need to be taken into account.

International movement of chemicals through trade or the environment can be important from the point of view of chemical control. The discussion internationally of these issues is at an early stage, and it is premature to seek generalized solutions, though progress can be made even now by studying specific opportunities on an issue-by-issue basis. For example, it is difficult to understand why label warnings about hazard used within one market should not now also be required on exports, in a form that meets the information needs of foreign users. Where chemicals are significantly restricted or banned for use in their countries of origin, it would appear reasonable for the exporting nation to provide an importing nation with the information it needs to make a timely assessment of risk in its own national context, and, to the extent that cooperation is sought, for the exporting nation to provide technical assistance in arriving at such judgments.

Many of the issues concerning the control of chemicals may require appropriate codification in the form of comprehensive international agreements. Though the ultimate need for such comprehensive agreements should be kept in mind as a long-term vehicle to resolve issues for which it is now premature to seek definitive solutions, step-by-step action on particular points begins the process of defining more general solutions. Thus, resolution of issues that can practically be dealt with not only establishes a record of achievement but builds the momentum toward more comprehensive agreements in the future.

References

Chapter I—Introduction

1. World Health Organization (WHO), International Agency for Research on Cancer (IARC), *Chemicals and Industrial Processes Associated with Cancer in Humans*, IARC Monographs on the Evaluation of the Carcinogenic Risk of Chemicals to Humans, September 1979, p. 12.

2. National Academy of Sciences (NAS), *Protection Against Depletion of Stratospheric Ozone by Chlorofluorocarbons* (Washington, D.C.: National Academy of Sciences, 1979), pp. 1-7.

3. U.S. Environmental Protection Agency, "TSCA Chemical Substances Inventory," *Administration of the Toxic Substances Control Act (1979)*, July 1980, p. 4.

4. U.S., Council on Environmental Quality (CEQ), *Environmental Quality: The Tenth Annual Report* (Washington, D.C.: U.S. Government Printing Office, December 1979), pp. 198-99.

5. National Academy of Sciences, *Chlorofluorocarbons*, pp. 41-42.

6. Sam Gusman, *Training Scientists for Future Toxic Substances Problems* (Washington, D.C.: The Conservation Foundation, 1978), pp. 7-8.

7. World Health Organization, IARC, *Cancer in Humans*, p. 12.

8. Organisation for Economic Cooperation and Development (OECD), Special Programme on the Control of Chemicals: Chemicals Group, "The International Control of Chemicals within the OECD Context," Paris, November 7, 1979. (ENV/CHEM/79.22)

9. Risebrough, "Chlorinated Hydrocarbons in Antarctic Birds," a paper presented at public hearings on DDT, U.S. Environmental Protection Agency, 1971-2.

10. "Facts and Figures for the Chemical Industry," *Chemical and Engineering News*, Vol. 58, No. 23, June 9, 1980, p. 71.

11. United Nations, Environment Programme, *IRPTC Bulletin*, Vol. 3, No. 1, January 1980, p. 15.

12. United Nations, Governing Council of UNEP, a presentation on the International Programme on Chemical Safety by a representative of the World Health Organization, April 23, 1980; United Nations, International Programme on Chemical Safety, *Proposed Activities 1980/81*.

13. "Facts and Figures," *Chemical and Engineering News*, p. 71.

14. U.S., Federal Insecticide, Fungicide, and Rodenticide Act (FIFRA), 7 U.S.C. 135 *et seq.*

15. U.S., Federal Food, Drug and Cosmetic Act, 21 U.S.C. 301-392 (1938, as amended).

16. U.S., Clean Air Act, 42 U.S.C. 1857 *et seq.*

17. U.S., Congress, Senate, Committee on Commerce, *The Toxic Substances Act of 1971 and Amendment S. 1478*, 92nd Congress, 1st Session, 1972.

18. U.S., Congress, House, Committee on Interstate and Foreign Commerce, *Toxic Substances Control Legislation—1973 HR 5087, HR 5356, HR 1014,* 93rd Congress, 1st Session, 1973.
19. U.S. Congress, House, Committee on Interstate and Foreign Commerce, *Legislative History of the Toxic Substances Control Act,* December 1976, pp. 668-69.
20. European Community, *Official Journal of the European Communities,* 76/907/EEC, Annex I, III, IV, Vol. 19, No. L 360, December 30, 1976.

Chapter II—Context

1. U.S., Administrative Procedure Act, 5 U.S.C., Section 551 *et seq.*
2. U.S., Freedom of Information Act, 5 U.S.C., Sec. 552.
3. Konrad von Moltke, "Europäische Umweltpolitik," *Zeitschrift für Umweltpolitik,* January 1979, pp. 77-92.
4. U.S. Environmental Protection Agency, *Initial Report of the TSCA Interagency Testing Committee to the Administrator,* October 1, 1977, pp. 4-16.

Chapter III—Assessing Hazard

1. Sam Gusman, *Training Scientists for Future Toxic Substances Problems* (Washington, D.C.: The Conservation Foundation, 1978), p. 5.
2. U.S., Council on Environmental Quality (CEQ), *Environmental Quality: The Tenth Annual Report* (Washington, D.C.: U.S. Government Printing Office, December 1979), pp. 188-196.
3. Ibid., p. 199.
4. J. L. Steinfeld, Testimony Before the Senate Committee on Commerce, Subcommittee on Energy, Natural Resources and Environment, August 27, 1970.
5. Organisation for Economic Cooperation and Development, Environment Committee, Chemicals Group, Chemicals Testing Programme, Expert Group Reports on: *Step Systems Group-Preliminary Report,* November 1979; *Degradation/Accumulation,* Vol. I, II, December 1979; *Environmental Effects,* Vol. I, II, III, December 1979; *Physical Chemistry,* Vol. I. II, December 1979; *Short Term and Long Term Toxicology,* December 1979; *Good Laboratory Practices,* March 1980.
6. OECD, Expert Group Report on *Degradation/Accumulation,* Vol. I, pp. 10-11.
7. OECD, Expert Group Report on *Short Term and Long Term Toxicology Groups,* pp. 25-29.
8. Edward Calabrase, *Pollutants and High Risk Groups* (New York: John Wiley and Sons, 1978).
9. Robert Friedman, *Sensitive Populations and Environmental Standards: A Legal Analysis* (Washington, D.C.: The Conservation Foundation, 1980).
10. U.S., Toxic Substances Strategy Committee, *Toxic Chemicals and Public Protection* (Washington, D.C.: U.S. Government Printing Office, May 1980), p. 125.
11. Joyce McCann and Bruce Ames, "Detection of Carcinogens as Mutagens in the Salmonella Microsome Test; Assay of 300 Chemicals: Discussion," *Proceedings of the National Academy of Sciences,* Vol. 73, 1976.
12. F. Sigmura, et al., "Overlapping of Carcinogens and Mutagens," *Fundamentals in Cancer Prevention* (Baltimore: University Park Press, 1976).
13. OECD, Expert Group Report on *Physical Chemistry,* Vol. 1, Appendix, 2.5.5.
14. OCED, Expert Group Report on *Short Term and Long Term Toxicology,* p. 23.

15. This description of ecotoxicological testing is largely based on the *Report on the Assessment of Potential Environmental Effects of Chemicals: the Effects on Organisms other than Man and on Ecosystems,* OECD Chemicals Testing Programme Ecotoxicology Group, December 1979.

16. "Organisation for Economic Cooperation and Development; Draft Agenda for High Level Meeting 19 May 1980 and Draft Decisions on the OECD Chemicals Program," *International Environmental Reporter,* Vol. 3, No. 5, May 14, 1980, pp. 211-12.

17. "Approaches for Developing Testing Guidelines Under the Toxic Substances Control Act," The Conservation Foundation, 1978, pp. 3-4. Unpublished.

18. OECD, Expert Group on *Short Term and Long Term Toxicology,* pp. 19-20.

19. Federal Republic of Germany, Law on Protection against Hazardous Substances (Chemicals Act), June 7, 1979. Draft.

20. *Federal Register,* Vol. 41, No. 225, November 19, 1976, p. 51208; U.S. Food and Drug Administration, Regulations for Good Laboratory Practice, 43 FR 59986, December 22, 1978.

21. U.S., *Federal Register,* Vol. 44, May 9, 1979, p. 27363.

22. "OECD: Draft Agenda for High Level Meeting 19 May 1980" *International Environmental Reporter,* pp. 206-210.

23. "Approaches for Developing Testing Guidelines."

24. "Accord Reached at OECD Meeting on Premarket Testing, 100 Test Guidelines," *Chemical Regulation Reporter,* Vol. 4, No. 9, May 30, 1980, pp. 204-205.

25. "EPA participation in reimbursement should be minimized, industry says," *Chemical Regulation Reporter,* Vol. 3, No. 46, February 15, 1980, pp. 1715-7.

26. [J. Clarence Davies and Frances Irwin], *Product Regulation and Chemical Innovation,* The Conservation Foundation, March 1980, p. II-23. Unpublished.

27. U.S., Senate, Committee on Commerce, Hearings Before the Environmental Subcommittee, 93rd Congress, 1st Session, 1973, p. 302.

28. U.S., House, Committee on Interstate and Foreign Commerce, Report together with Minority Views, 96th Congress, 2nd Session, 1980, p. 18.

Chapter IV—Notification Requirements

1. U.S. Environmental Protection Agency, "Toxic Substances Control: Inventory Reporting Requirements," *Federal Register,* Vol. 42, No. 247, December 23, 1977.

2. U.S. Environmental Protection Agency, "Premanufacture Notification Requirements and Review Procedures," *Federal Register,* Vol. 44, No. 7, January 10, 1979.

3. "Reproposal of TSCA PMN Forms and Provisions of Rules," *Federal Register,* Vol. 44, No. 201, October 16, 1979.

4. U.S., House, Committee on Interstate and Foreign Commerce, Report together with Minority Views, 96th Congress, 2nd Session, 1980, p. 18.

5. J. P. Parenteau, Personal Communication, 1980.

6. U.S. Environmental Protection Agency, *Impact of TSCA Proposed Premanufacturing Notification Requirements,* prepared by Arthur D. Little, Inc., December 1978, pp. VI-3 & 4.

7. U.S. Environmental Protection Agency, "Toxic Substances Control: Inventory Reporting Requirements," *Federal Register,* Vol. 42, No. 247, December 23, 1977, p. 64573.

8. U.S. Environmental Protection Agency, "Reproposal of PMN Forms," October 16, 1979, p. 59770.

9. European Community, Council Directive on the disposal of polychlorinated biphenyls and polychlorinated terphenyls (76/403/EEC) (OJ No. L 108, April 26, 1976), p. 41;

Council Directive on the approximation of the laws of the Member States relating to materials and articles which contain vinyl chloride monomer and are intended to come into contact with foodstuffs (78/142/EEC) (OJ No. L 44, February 15, 1978), p. 15.

10. "Organisation for Economic Cooperation and Development; Draft Agenda for High Level Meeting 19 May 1980 and Draft Decisions on the OECD Chemicals Program" *International Environmental Reporter*, Vol. 3, No. 5, May 14, 1980, p. 217.

11. European Community, *Official Journal of the European Communities*, C 260, November 5, 1976.

Chapter V—Risk Assessment and Control

1. Loi No. 77-771 du 12 juillet 1977 sur le contrôle des produits chimiques (JO du 13 juillet 1977, p. 3801) English summary translation: Commonwealth Law Bulletin, Vol. 4, No. 2, April 1978; Lov om kemiske stoffer og produkter (Lov. nr. 212 af 23 maj 1979) Translation available from Ministry of the Environment, Denmark.

2. U.S. Environmental Protection Agency, *Chemical Use Classification System*, Auerbach Associates, Inc., October 1977. (EPA-560/9-77-001)

3. "Setting Priorities for Chemicals under the Toxic Substances Control Act," The Conservation Foundation, August 1977, p. 14. Unpublished.

4. National Academy of Sciences, *Protection Against Depletion of Stratospheric Ozone by Chlorofluorocarbons* (Washington, D.C.: National Academy of Sciences, 1979), pp. 123-270.

5. Décret No. 79-35 du 15 janvier 1979 sur le contrôle des produits chimiques (JO du 17 janvier 1979, p. 148).

6. Rapport sur le projet de loi de finances pour 1978, Annexe 6, Environnement, par M. Marcellin, Sénat, Doc No. 88.

7. J. Clarence Davies, Sam Gusman and Frances Irwin, *Determining Unreasonable Risk under the Toxic Substances Control Act* (Washington, D.C.: The Conservation Foundation, 1979).

8. U.S., Nuclear Regulatory Commission Task Force, *Proposed Goals for Nuclear Waste Treatment*, 1976.

9. U.S. Environmental Protection Agency, Proceedings of a Workshop on Issues Pertinent to the Development of Environmental Criteria for Radioactive Wastes, Reston, Virginia, 1977.

10. C. Vlek and P. J. Stallen, *Statistische Beschrijving en Persoonlijke Beleving Van Risico's Voor de Bevolking in een Geindustrialiseerd Gebied* (Den Haag: Koninklijk Instituut van Ingenieurs, 1979).

11. Ibid.; P. Slovik, B. Fischhoff, and S. Lichenstein, "Rating the Risks," *Environment*, Vol. 21, No. 3, 1979, p. 19.

12 Chauncey Starr, "Benefit-Cost Studies in Sociotechnical Systems," *Perspectives on Benefit-Risk Decision Making*, (Washington, D.C.: National Academy of Engineering, 1973).

Chapter VI—International Trade

1. "Facts and Figures for the Chemical Industry," *Chemical & Engineering News*, Vol. 58, No. 23, June 9, 1980, p. 34.

2. "Organisation for Economic Cooperation and Development: Draft Agenda for High Level Meeting 19 May 1980 and Draft Decisions on the OECD Chemicals Program," *International Environment Reporter*, Vol. 3, No. 5, May 14, 1980, p. 214.

3. U.S., CEQ/EPA/Department of Commerce, *Economic Impact of Pollution Control* (Washington, D.C.: U.S. Government Printing Office, 1972); Estimates by The Conference Board, New York, 1976, Unpublished; Ingo Walter, "The Pollution Content of American Trade," *Western Economic Journal,* March 1973; John H. Mutti and J. David Richardson, "International Competitive Displacement from Environmental Control: The Quantitative Gains from Methodological Refinement," *Journal of Environmental Economics and Management,* June 1977.

4. General Agreement on Tariffs and Trade (GATT), Articles of Agreement and Related Documents, Geneva: 1977.

5. GATT, "Agreement on Technical Barriers to Trade," Geneva: April 12, 1979.

6. European Court of Justice, Decision of March 31, 1971.

7. U.S., Comments of the American Importers Association on the Regulations proposed pursuant to Section 8(a) of the Toxic Substances Control Act, May 9, 1977.

8. Eastman Kodak Company, Further Comments on Supplemental Notice to Proposed Inventory Reporting Requirements, February 13, 1978.

9. For a more extensive discussion of the siting of production facilities, see J. Leonard, "Environment and International Industrial Siting Policy" and J. Leonard and C. Duerksen, "Environmental Regulations and the Location of Industry: An International Perspective," papers presented for a Conservation Foundation Conference on the Role of Environmental and Land-Use Regulation in Industrial Siting, June, 1979.

Chapter VII—Transfer of Information

1. Organisation for Economic Cooperation and Development, "Technology on Trial: Public Participation in Decision-Making Related to Science and Technology," Paris, 1979.

2. Renate Mayntz, *Vollzugsprobleme der Umweltpolitik Materialien zur Umweltforschung* (Wiesbaden: Rat von Sachverständigen für Umweltfragen, 1978).

3. U.S., Toxic Substances Strategy Committee, *Toxic Chemicals and Public Protection* (Washington, D.C.: U.S. Government Printing Office, May 1980), pp. iv-v.

4. Ibid., p. 38-39.

5. Ibid., p. 38-42.

6. U.S., Interagency Regulatory Liaison Group, *Proposed Minimum Standards for the Protection of Confidential Business Information shared by CPSC, EPA, FDA, OSHA,* 1978.

7. "Court Grants Polaroid Injunction—Questions TSCA Disclosure Provisions," *Chemical Regulation Reporter,* Vol. 2, No. 13, June 30, 1978, pp. 423-4. "Polaroid Dismisses TSCA Lawsuits, Is Satisfied with Security Rules," *Chemical Regulation Reporter,* Vol. 2, No. 32, November 10, 1978, p. 1389.

8. U.S., Federal Insecticide, Fungicide, and Rodenticide Act (FIFRA), 7 U.S.C. 136.

9. U.S. Environmental Protection Agency, Freedom of Information Act Procedures, 40 C.F.R. §2.301(h).

10. U.S., Toxic Substances Strategy Committee, *Toxic Chemicals,* pp. 41-42.

11. Beiträge zur Beurteilung der Umweltwirksamkeit chemischer Stoffe (Bonn: Deutsche Forschungsgemeinschaft, Senatsausschuss für Umweltforschung, 1979).

12. Senato del la republica, documenti di seduta 1978 and 1979 contain summary minutes of the Commission's meetings indicating who was heard.

13. Süddeutsche Zeitung, 12 August 1978.

14. S. P. Johnson, *The Pollution Control Policies of the European Community* (Graham and Trolman, 1979).

15. "Organisation for Economic Cooperation and Development: Draft Agenda for High Level Meeting 19 May 1980 and Draft Decisions on the OECD Chemicals Program," *International Environmental Reporter,* Vol. 3, No. 5, May 14, 1980, p. 214.

16. Bracken, et al., Chemical Substances Information Network, June 1977.

17. United Nations, Environmental Programme, IRPTC Bulletin, Vol. 3, No. 1, January 1980, pp. 6-8.

18. American National Standards Institute 129.1-1976, September 1976.

19. Sam Gusman and Frances Irwin, *Chemical Hazard Warnings: Labeling for Effective Communication* (Washington, D.C.: The Conservation Foundation, 1979).

20. "Appendix A: Instructions for Asserting and Substantiating Claims of Confidentiality," *Chemical Regulation Reporter,* Vol. 3, No. 29, October 19, 1979, pp. 1223-1238; U.S. Environmental Protection Agency, *Freedom of Information Act Requests: Confidentiality of Business Information,* 40 CFR Part 2, as amended, 1979.

21. Virginia, Toxic Substances Information Act Regulations: Rules and Regulations for the Reporting of Chemical Substances Manufactured and Used in Manufactirng, §8.02, October 1, 1979.

22. Loi du E Loi No. 78-753 du 29 juillet 1978 sur l'accès des citoyens aux documents administratifs (JO du 18 juillet 1978, p. 2851).

23. See, for example, Philadelphia Area Project on Occupational Safety and Health (Philaposh) "Chronology of Right to Know Campaign, 1970-79" prepared for the Delaware Valley Toxics Coalition.

Chapter VIII—Policy Options: Harmonization and Implementation

1. Recommendation No. 74 of the UN Conference on the Human Environment in Stockholm, 1972, which called for international acceptability of procedures for testing pollutants and contaminants.

2. Two OECD Council Recommendations, 1974 and 1977, which called for "The Assessment of the Potential Environmental Effects of Chemicals" and Guidelines in Respect of Procedures and Requirements for Anticipating the Effects of Chemicals on Man and the Environment.

Appendix I

Contributing Authors

Dr. A. Karim Ahmed
Senior Staff Scientist
Natural Resources Defense Council, U.S.A.

Congressman Bob Eckhardt
House of Representatives, U.S.A.

Dr. Sam Gusman
Senior Associate
The Conservation Foundation, U.S.A.

Ms. Marietta Idman-Philp
Formerly of the Organisation for Economic Cooperation
and Development

Ms. Frances Irwin
Associate
The Conservation Foundation, U.S.A.

Mr. Stanley P. Johnson
Vice Chairman, Committee on the Environment, Public Health,
and Consumer Protection, The European Parliament

Mr. Jean-Paul Parenteau
Chef du Service du Contrôle des Produits
Ministère de l'Environnement et du Cadre de Vie, France

Dr. Lucas Reijnders
Centre for Environmental Studies
University of Groningen, The Netherlands

Dr. E. M. B. Smith
Senior Medical Officer
Department of Health and Social Security,
United Kingdom

Dr. Ingo Walter
Professor
Graduate School of Business Administration
New York University, U.S.A.

Appendix II
Advisory Committee

Mr. Goffredo del Bino
Principal Administrator
Commission of the European Communities
Environment and Consumer Protection Service

Ms. Frances Charlesworth
Department of the Environment, United Kingdom

Dr. Peter Crawford
Head of the Chemical Products Division
Organisation for Economic Cooperation and Development

Dr. J. Clarence Davies III
Executive Vice President
The Conservation Foundation, U.S.A.

Mr. George S. Dominguez
Director of Government Relations, Safety, Health and Ecology
CIGA-GEIGY Corporation, U.S.A.

Congressman Bob Eckhardt
House of Representatives, U.S.A.

Mr. Irving L. Fuller
Director for International Chemical Affairs
Office of Pesticides and Toxic Substances
Environmental Protection Agency, U.S.A.

Mr. Steven Jellinek
Assistant Administrator for Toxic Substances
Environmental Protection Agency, U.S.A.

Mr. Joergen Henningsen
Miljøstyrelsen, Denmark

Mr. ir. Jan V. Henselmans
Stichting Natuur en Milieu, The Netherlands

Mr. Stanley P. Johnson
Vice Chairman, Committee on the Environment, Public Health,
and Consumer Protection
The European Parliament

Dr. Ing. Arno Katin
Ministerialrat
Bundesministerium des Innern,
Federal Republic of Germany

Mr. Rune Lönngren
National Products Control Board, Sweden

Mr. Jean-Paul Parenteau
Chef du Service du Contrôle des Produits
Ministère de l'Environnement et du Cadre de Vie, France

Dr. Glenn Paulson
Vice President for Science
National Audubon Society, U.S.A.

Dr. P. L. de Reeder
International Coordinator Environment
Akzo, The Netherlands

Dr. Eckard Rehbinder
Professor of Trade Regulation and Environmental Law
University of Frankfurt, Federal Republic of Germany

Mr. Robert A. Roland
President
Chemical Manufacturers Association, U.S.A.

Dr. Martin Uppenbrink
Direktor beim
Umweltbundesamt, Federal Republic of Germany

The Authors

Sam Gusman is a senior associate at The Conservation Foundation. He is responsible for the Foundation's program of research, analysis, and mediation on environmental issues related to chemicals.

Konrad von Moltke is director of the Institute for European Environmental Policy. The Institute, based in Paris and Bonn, is an independent nonprofit center for the critical analysis of strategies and alternatives for dealing with environmental problems in Europe.

Frances Irwin is an associate in The Conservation Foundation's pollution and toxic substances control program. She has a particular interest in citizen education projects.

Cynthia Whitehead is The Conservation Foundation's staff representative in Europe. Based in Bonn, she conducts research on land use and environmental policy.